You Can Do All Things

By Dr. Jake Schmitz

Disclaimer and Copyright Notification:

ISBN: 0692295003
ISBN-13: 978-0692295007

DEDICATION

You can do all things is dedicated to my lovely wife Mikala and my son Jesyn.

You two anchor me and help me be a better person each day. You inspire me to always be my best self. Thank you for believing in me and for helping me believe in myself. I love you both very much.

CONTENTS

ACKNOWLEDGMENTS

First, a huge thank you to my sister Codi for all the work she put in to make this the best book possible.

You donated hours upon hours to this project with no expectation of a return. I appreciate you endlessly and am thankful to have you in my life.

Second, an equally large thank you goes out to Faye. You have given me nothing but encouragement since day one. You always speak to my potential and you have always made me feel loved. Thank you for all the work you did for me on this book. It means the world to me to know you are here for my family.

Lastly, a big thank you goes out to my team at FCHC, my awesome patients that pushed me to write this book, and anyone else that has helped me along the way. You are valued more than you know!

INTRODUCTION

I wrote *You Can Do All Things* because I have seen many patients with recurring problems in their life that keep holding them down. I thought if they could just get past their issue or situation, they would be able to get on with life and move towards becoming their best possible selves. That being said, I also realized that I did not have the appropriate amount of time to devote to individual mentoring and counseling. I have one of the largest alternative healthcare practices in the upper Midwest. I see around 12,000 to 15,000 patients each year in my office. I only have a couple of minutes per patient, and some of them really needed the time and mentoring to move past their limitation. I was getting frustrated with this dichotomy...too much to say and not enough time to say it! That was what pushed me to write *You Can Do All Things*. I knew that if I could put a resource in my patients' hands, more could be accomplished with less time so that they could have the amazing transformation in their lives, without the one-on-one time it was consistently taking. You will hear some of my patients' stories throughout this book. Their stories are used to drive home the power of the principles that you are about to learn!

I am not a counselor! I do not have any advanced degrees in psychology! If you have watched the movie *Taken* with Liam Neeson, you probably remember every person's favorite quote. Liam Neeson tells the bad guys who kidnapped his daughter about himself. He says, "What I do have are a very particular set of skills acquired over a very long career…" That describes me perfectly. I have a very specialized set of skills that have been acquired over years of working with thousands of patients. I have not seen it all, but pretty close!

I am frequently asked by patients, "how do you always know exactly what I needed to hear?" I usually tell them, "it is easy…I just had that conversation with someone else yesterday!"

Experience is the best instructor. I have done hundreds of group presentations for tens of thousands of people. Whether it was in dozens of churches across the country, corporations large and small, or workshops in my office, I have seen transformation through these simple principles and exercises. They work!

Whether you are willing to let them work for you is the real question. If you apply these lessons in your life, you will be changed forever! I have seen this to be true thousands of times, and you will see it as well. So, go ahead and dive in! It will be fun for you and also a life-altering experience!

What stops you from being the person God has called you to be? Is it fear? Regret? Self-confidence issues? Self-esteem? Skills? Talent? Ability? Some combination of these issues? Or something else entirely? Whatever it is, the first step to overcoming is diagnosing! You have to diagnose the "problem," or the thing or group of things holding you back from becoming who God has called you to be. Once you diagnose the mental blockade that is keeping you from pursuing your dreams, fulfillment is right around the corner! You are closer to your dreams than you ever imagined. You just have to get the heck out of your own way! You are the only person who can stop you from hitting your goals and accomplishing your mission! It doesn't matter what your parents think or that friend who you don't really like anyway or some school teacher or co-worker. What matters most is what you think! How does what you think line up with what God wants for your life? The moment those two things--what you want for your life and what God wants for your life--lineup, life transformation happens and your biggest dreams come true.

3

The purpose of *You Can Do All Things* is to act as a guide. Every person is different, so people come to me with different problems. What is consistent, however, is the path to overcoming these problems. Some people have trouble getting over past hurts. Some people cannot shake an experience they had when they were young. Others are struggling with a lack of confidence that is holding them back. The reason I decided to write this resource manual was to help bridge the gap for those people who are being hindered in their life by something that can and should be overcome!

Help is a requirement to make it through this life! We have all been there. You remember both ends, I suspect. You remember being the person who needed the help and also being the support system for someone else struggling with issues. I have heard it stated best as we are either in a storm, coming out of a storm, or about to go into one! Problems are always there, but how we are able to overcome those problems will be the key to lasting success, abundance, prosperity, overwhelming peace, and quality relationships in life!

Are you coming out a storm or heading into one? Or, are you in the midst of the storm of your life and not sure how to come out of it? *You Can Do All Things* was written for you! In this book you will be given the tools, keys, strategies, and advice on how to create the life of your dreams. This book is based on hundreds of best-selling books, numerous self-help gurus, clinical experience, and personal experience. I know it can help you become the best person within your ultimate design!

You Can Do All Things has been broken up into three parts for easy digestion. Part one is about "Diagnosing the Problem" or problems that are interfering with your dreams. For the majority of people, your fear is your biggest obstacle keeping you from greatness. The starting point for you will be deciphering which type of fear is holding you back. The five main fears that consistently rear their ugly heads each have their own section. Your mission is to establish which fear is attacking you. When you understand where your fear is rooted, then you can change and adapt your behavior to overcome that fear.

For some, it is not fear that is your crutch, but a SELF issue! Whether it is self-confidence or self-esteem (yes, they are two entirely different things!), you will get the exercises you need to flex that mental muscle to develop more of what you are lacking! After developing the skills discussed in these chapters, you will then be able to step into the person you were born to be!

For others, your skills, talent, or ability is what is keeping you down. In those chapters, you will be given the tools to ensure that you can and will start the journey to self improvement! The most important concept is when you can diagnose the problem, then you can take the mask off the monster and realize the thing holding you back is actually you!

Part two is "Cultivating Your Character." Success leaves clues! What are the action steps that all successful people do in order to achieve massive success? In this part, we will walk through what positive habits these successful people have in common. Their success came AFTER they cultivated these characteristics! You will understand how to develop the discipline necessary to unlock your greatest achievements! After you learn the discipline habits, I will teach you how to set goals. Up until now, you have had WISHES, but not GOALS! You will learn the best way to set goals with the expectation of successfully accomplishing them! Lastly, you will learn to strengthen your greatest asset...YOUR MIND!! The processes of affirmations and visualizations have been used by thousands of people in every sector or industry for the last 500 years! You have a goal or dream, and that is a great start. In order to achieve that dream, you have to go through a process of change to become the person who can accomplish his/her dream.

In this part, we will look at attributes necessary to overcome challenges and what kind of character is needed to be a champion!

Part three is "Delivering the Goods." After "Diagnosing the Problem" and "Cultivating Your Character," now you will work on "Delivering the Goods" to embrace your purpose on this planet. We will look at several successful people and their journey to greatness. What did they do to have a lasting impact on humanity? The bigger your dream, the bigger your impact needs to be! How did these people leave a gigantic legacy for posterity? How can you do the same? The clues are there for you to grab hold of and run with...are you willing to do it?

Once you've completed reading this book, you will have no more reason to stay the same. You will be a different person! You will have changed into who God has called you to be! You will start completing your goals, on a path to the top of your industry. You'll be transformed into the best version of yourself. You will become the person your spouse knew you could be. You will become the parent your kids deserve. You will be recognized by your employer for the amazing work you are doing. You'll earn all the accolades you are striving for because you will be in line with the person God created!

Have I got your attention yet? Good! Now keep reading to become the Master of your own destiny!

PART 1

DIAGNOSING THE PROBLEM

CHAPTER 1

FEAR WILL PARALYZE YOU

"Fear cuts deep than swords."
~ George R.R. Martin

The most common and most consistent reason people have for not achieving their goals, fulfilling their God-ordained purpose, and accumulating wealth and success is fear. Five fears are routinely cited as barriers that stand in the way of people reaching their full potential. However, fear does not discriminate. It comes in all shapes and sizes and wears many faces, so if your fear is not mentioned on this list, do not worry. The principles for overcoming fears are the same. So no matter what your fear is, if you follow these guidelines, you can silence that voice in your head telling you to be afraid!

Failure

The fear of failure is definitely the most common doubt people say they have to work through on a daily, weekly, or monthly basis. Often I find this fear is rooted in past failures. As humans, we associate past feelings with expectations of things to come. We play small with our goals and dreams because we have an unsubstantiated fear of failure. We look back at all the things we have tried before, like sports, work, and family interactions, and then extrapolate those past events into future settings.

Let's look at a real-life example of a person who was struggling with the fear of failure. Kelly couldn't get past her fear. She suffered so much that she was having physical symptoms due to her fear! She was so scared; she wouldn't even leave her house because of the anxiety that came with her fear. She was in her twenties and living a life that was less than her potential. She would go to work and then go home. She did not have any social life because of the fear. I met Kelly at a church event I held in North Carolina. It was very evident that Kelly was struggling with past failures that had crept into her current reality. I helped her see that the past is exactly that, the past! I told her that nothing from the past can hurt her unless she lets it. After some time, she was able to let go of the past failures and hurts and finally move on. Once freed from this fear, she was able to return to a normal life! She worked with her doctor and came off half a dozen medications for anxiety and depression. Now, she is happily married and living the life she always dreamt of living!

Kelly's story is a perfect example of how these principles can help you overcome anything that is holding you back! Here are some more examples to give you an idea of how this works.

"I can't get a good grade in school because the last time I tried, it didn't work. Why bother this time?"

"I won't achieve success at work because last year I tried taking on extra responsibility and I dropped the ball. I will not try that again!"

"Last year I went out for the team and embarrassed myself, so this year I won't go out for the team."

The examples are simple ways in which we let the fear overrule our dreams. I would be willing to bet you have a couple of these in your life! The first step to overcoming fear is to identify. Write them out as I have above. When you see them written out, you can paint a clear picture in your mind of what is holding you back. Once identified, the healing process can begin.

You have to visualize fear like a disease. Diseases, categorically, are slow-acting. They fester. Gradually, over many years, a disease eats away at the surrounding tissue until all that is left is the disease itself. If it is left to its own devices, a disease will kill you slowly over many years. Fortunately for us, we have a supercharged system in place. Our immune system is there to target and eliminate any disease immediately after the disease starts. Picture a Navy seal sniper team! They eliminate the bad guy before he even knows they are there! But what happens when the immune system does not find the disease? That's right; it overruns the body!

In that scenario, fear is the disease, and your mind is the immune system, a Navy seal. You have the power to take out your fear before it has a chance to run wild. You can, and should, crush your fear before it gets traction. Eliminate it before it can get a grip on your psyche. Unfortunately, too many people minimize their fear. We, by tendency, think our problems are always smaller than they really are for us. We blow off the voice in our head telling us there is a problem. We know we should deal with it right away. But, what do we tell ourselves? We convince ourselves that it isn't a big deal, or maybe we will deal with it later, or it will not affect our lives, but we know the truth! If we could do a better job listening to the voice, we could avoid a lot of needless suffering! Unfortunately, in the majority of cases I see, that is just not the case. We are reactive instead of proactive. Most people wait until they have an issue arise before dealing with the problem.

The best example I can use for this is in healthcare. If you consistently eat the wrong foods (sugary treats, simple carbohydrates, candy, etc.,) you will mess up your blood sugar. When your doctor tells you to change, stating that you are now in the class of pre-diabetic due to your eating habits, you have a choice. You can either change your habits, which will reverse your situation, or you can continue down the path of diabetes. Many people ignore their doctor's advice and keep making the same decisions. Those are the same people who are surprised when the doctor tells them they are now diabetic! They should not have been surprised at all, since the doctor told them to change or suffer the consequences! The point of this example is that you are at a crossroads. You can change, eliminate the fear, or else let it fester to the point where it is a disease. Make the right choice! Follow this path to wipe out your fear. You will be happy you did!

Now that you have identified your past failure that has anchored itself in your subconscious, we can learn the lesson it is still trying to teach you. What are your past failures trying to tell you? Once you learn a lesson, you can move on to a better future, and you can let go of what has been holding you back for years, or even decades in some cases. Let's look at the lessons the previous examples are trying to teach us.

"I can't get the good grade in school because the last time I tried, it didn't work. Why bother this time?"

Our minds, by nature, have a hard time comprehending those things we are merely interested in. The mind focuses harder on those topics or events that we have an active interest in. When the interest level goes down, the mind stops focusing and as a result the grades (in this example) suffer as well. If you, or maybe your children, have this issue, and you try hard to overcome, it still might not be enough on your own. Unfortunately, with our system the way it is today, you do not get the excuse that you are disinterested in a topic. You still (or your children) have to pass your classes. Try a tutor! The job of the tutor is to find positive ways to engage your brain to make it interesting and engaging for you. In this example, the lesson to learn is ask for help! Don't try to do everything on your own. Once you identify your tendencies, you can make the necessary corrections.

"I won't achieve success at work because last year I tried taking on extra responsibility and I dropped the ball. I will not try that again!"

So many people fall into this trap. You try to extend yourself in an effort to stand out, and all that happened is you got so over-extended that you unraveled at the seams! If this is you, don't worry. You are in good company! Every person who achieves success has had this feeling at some point in the journey. So, what is the lesson that needs to be learned here? Last time I calculated, a day only lasts 24 hours. That will never change. Typically, the average work day is eight hours. That, for the most part, will not change either. That being said, if you have eight hours of responsibilities that you need to accomplish every day, with only eight hours to do it, you do not have any more time for extra work. Since you cannot change the amount of time you have to get the job done, what can you do? You have two options. Either you can get better i.e. increase your skills, or delegate to someone else! I will come back to training as it relates to increasing your skills. The lesson for this example is delegation. The one thing all massively successful people have in common is delegating the small things to other people. How do you choose what to delegate to someone else? A general rule is if it (your responsibility) is something that can be done by someone else to increase your productivity with jobs requiring more skills or training, then shift it to someone else who is capable. If you are the only one with the skills to do the job, then it is classified as an essential role, and you are the only one to do it. By delegating non-essential roles, you will not only increase your effectiveness (get more done in less time) but also empower those people around you to take on more responsibilities. In that regard, your workplace will start accomplishing more, which will impress your boss, and potentially land you the promotion you have been waiting to get!

Another example of this is within your home. If your home is like mine, husband spends his day at the office and wife spends her day raising the kids and taking care of the house (this can be interchanged, where the husband is home and wife is at work). My wife Mikala can get a ton of cleaning and child rearing done without any help of mine. She is only one person, however, and there are times when she cannot get everything done, like when family or friends are coming to stay, or when students are coming to shadow my practice. In times such as those, Mikala will delegate household chores to me in an effort to double our efficiency. If the spouse absolutely cannot help because he is gone, then your older children work well as a substitute! Delegation is a skill that can and should be used often to increase your effectiveness and get more done with less time!

"Last year I went out for the team and embarrassed myself, so this year I will not go out for the team."

My response to this is simple. When you went out for the team last year, how much did you practice before the tryouts? According to Malcolm Gladwell's book *Outliers*, to become a master at anything takes approximately 10,000 hours of practice. Therefore, if you want to be good at something, you need to train! I will devote an entire chapter to this, at this time I will ask you one question; how badly do you want it? Rate yourself on a scale from 0 to 10. 0 is you do not want it at all; 10 is you want it more than you want to breathe. If you rate yourself less than eight, you do not want it badly enough. It is time to reevaluate. The lesson to learn is that in order to succeed, you have to be willing to improve your skill set!

What is the lesson your past failures are trying to tell you? Write them out and spend time meditating on them. What is the dominant feeling you have when thinking back to that moment? That emotion will tell you a lot about how you are responding in your current situation. More than likely, you are still allowing past failures to affect future situations. This self-analysis will allow you to recognize your weakness and overcome so you stop self-sabotaging. Once you are out of your own way, success will be your only possible result.

Success

Another fear, not quite as common as failure, is the fear of success. On the surface, this fear seems counterproductive. People with this fear are afraid of what success will do to them. They are actually scared to change for the better due to a disproportional fear of what they will be losing in the process. These people cannot visualize the good things that will happen when goals are met. They see the person they will have to become to hit their objective, and it scares them. Personally, this is one of my biggest fears I continually deal with on a yearly basis. For me, this fear lives in what would happen when my goals are achieved. The cycle in my head goes something like this.

Me Currently + Hard Work = Goals Met → **DIFFERENT ME ENTIRELY**

The thought process was the "Current Me" was not enough

to meet my goals. So, through hard work and effort, I would eventually hit my goals, but in the process, I would change into a completely different person. I was not scared of the hard work, and I definitely was not scared of hitting my goals. What scared me the most was the thought that I would become a different person in the process. My coaches kept telling me that to achieve success, you have to change who you are now into the better version of yourself that can succeed, because who you are now will not have what it takes to achieve success. I took that to heart. What scared me was not even the thought of changing. It was the realization that after I had changed, I could not go back to the old me. That was what terrified me. I liked the old me!

Maybe you can relate to this. You are not worried about the work it will take, and you are okay with failing in order to gain the knowledge necessary to grow, but you do not like the idea of who you will become after this process runs its course. If that is you, do not worry, you are in good company. What I will tell is going to encourage you and give you the hope you need to go for it, to make your dreams a reality! This fear is not so much what will happen when you change, but what will you lose in the process. Whether it is the amount of television or computer time you get each day, or going to the movies on weekends, or date night with your spouse, time with your children or something else entirely. Your fear of success, like mine, was not in the success, but in what I thought I would have to give up along the way. This, of course, was not, nor is not, a reflection of reality, but a projection of my unrealistic expectations and fear. The most important thing to remember is that no one can foresee the future! The only fear is an idea of a future where you have to endure pain without expectation of pleasure from current joyful experiences. One simple revelation will set you free from this fear. You will actually have more time, not less, when you develop yourself into the new version of you! How? In Chapter 6, I will be discussing the concept of war-planning, or schedule and time management. Once these skills are in place, you will have an ample amount of time for your favorite activities, which eliminates the fear you are harboring. With this fear gone, you are now free to explore new possibilities. You can pursue higher goals and aspirations now that you have unshackled yourself from the unrealistic future negative expectations you have been currently holding onto.

Work

Another view that inhibits people from reaching their dreams and aspirations is the fear of the work it will take to achieve victory in life. The trap you fall into with this fear is perception.

We, as a culture, have a perceived notion that to make it to the next level in business, family, life, etc., you will have a proportional increase in the amount of work you will have to do to get there. This sentiment, fortunately, is not a reality in the majority of cases. It is okay to take a sigh of relief when reading that last sentence!

To be clear, and in an attempt to avoid negligence, there will be an increase in your workload depending on the immensity of the goal at hand. If you are currently unemployed, and your goal is to earn $1 million this year, then you will have your work cut out for you! This goal is not impossible; you just have to get to work because currently, you are unemployed (zero work). In order to achieve your goal, you will need to do a lot of something or many little things (more than zero)! In that scenario, you can see work will increase. That is okay. How badly do you want success? How much are you willing to endure? Write down your answers to these questions; they will tell you where your motivation currently is and will expose the likelihood you have of hitting your goal. If your answer is less than where you wanted to be, one of two choices remains: restructure your goal to be more realistic to current circumstances or find the inspiration to push past your limiting mindset! Do not move on until you have your answer.

I am here to give you encouragement. For the vast majority of people reading this, you do not need any increase in your workload. All you need is more efficiency in your life, so you can do more with less time requirements. I will discuss the application of this when we go over war plans in Chapter 6. I want to walk through the mindset of highly successful people in this section. What I have found with every person who has achieved massive success in life is when they reached higher goals, typically, they had <u>more</u> time for family, social life, vacations, etc. rather than less! Highly successful people consistently share this commonality. These people are masters of time management! The only thing these successful people have that you might not currently possess is a mastery of their war plan. The only thing these people "sacrifice" from their life are the "time vampires." We all have "time vampires," or those things that suck away our time. For many people now it is Facebook, email, television, computer time, movies, etc. What is your time vampire? Chances are good that you already recognize yours. Some are subtle, 10 minutes here or 20 minutes there, but all those minutes add up. Some people waste hours a day on useless things that hold them back. How does any of this relate to the fear of the work it will take to achieve victory in life?

Remember, most of this fear is the notion or perception of

increased work over and above current standards of your workload. What would happen if I could help you see that, on average, you are wasting two to four hours a day doing things that are hurting your goals instead of helping them? Then, in seeing how you can redirect that time (or even a small portion of it) towards activities that will help you achieve your goal, you will actually save time instead of spending more, and also achieve your goal FASTER! How does that change your perception? Your fear should change from "how much extra work will it take to achieve success?" to "how much time am I currently wasting?" When you can make that switch in your mind, it is actually easy to overcome this fear. Chapter 6 will go over the steps to find out how to master your time. When you can master your time, nothing will be able to stop you. Write down all the things that are "time vampires." Now that you see them, start eliminating them, and see how much extra time you really have. Every successful person had to go through the process of time mastery in order to gain their next level of success. The good news is that everyone has to do it! The best time to start is now.

Time

Fear of time, just like the fear of work, is another perception-based fear that keeps you on the bench and away from fulfilling the promise of abundance and prosperity that you have the capacity of reaching. Fear of time and the fear of work have a lot of overlap. I will try to not repeat any information, but at its basic level, fear of time is another misguided perception of a future event that will, more than likely, never come to reality or fruition.

Jennifer comes to mind when I think of the fear of time. She was 24 years old when this happened. She was at my office and we were talking about her plans for life. She explained that because she was now healthier she should get a job and move on with her life. I asked her if she was going to finish school (she had taken a couple of years off due to health concerns.) She told me that she didn't think she should because she was already 24 years old and too old to go back to school. I looked right at Jennifer and asked her how old she would be when she graduated, all things working out the right way. She told me she would have to take about three more years of school to graduate. I told her that would mean she would be 27 years old. She said that sounded right. I asked at what age she wanted to retire. She said 60 years old. Laughing to myself, I asked her if there was much difference between 33 years of work and 36 years of work. Jennifer paused for a second, smiled, and said "I guess not!" Then, I asked if she would rather spend 33 years doing something she loved, or 36 years doing things that she didn't like as much, but gained three extra years? The answer was obvious! I asked her what was better, investing three years now into her best possible future, or working the extra three years because she thought she was running out of time? Again, the answer was obvious!

The fear of time works this way! We make all these assumptions as to not having enough time, or that time is running out. Sometimes we need someone to take a step back and give us a realistic viewpoint to help see the reality of the situation! That was what I did for Jennifer. She had a negative expectation of a future scenario where she was running out of time. That was not at all true! In what ways do you have that same fear?

We, as a society, let unrealistic, negative expectations of an undesired future dominate our conscious and subconscious until it cripples us and keeps us from pursuing our dreams! One fundamental truth needs to be explored as it pertains to this fear. The truth is that no one knows the future. We have a terrible habit of assuming the worst out of every situation. With this assumption, it becomes easy for us to not want to try new things or set new goals because we come up with five or ten reasons why they will not work. The fear of time is no different.

Let's explore the two main reasons people have when it

comes to the fear of time. People are afraid that it will either take too long to achieve their goal (months/years), or that they will lose too much of their personal time in order to achieve their goal (sacrificing one thing to gain another). I have already explained how to overcome the second part. Now we are going to walk through the steps to achieve success over time.

You only need two tools to overcome this aspect of the fear of time. The first one is to plan it out. Write out your goal or dream on paper. Then, decide realistically how long it should take, all things being considered. An example of this would be if you want to go to graduate school to study business and economics to become a consultant for a Fortune 500 company. Do the math on how long it should take you to achieve this goal. If you are currently a senior in high school, you first have to graduate. Then you need a four-year degree, which takes many people five years to achieve. Next, you need to make it through graduate school, which is another 2 years, leaving you with a goal that will take at least seven years to accomplish, assuming all things go perfectly for you. Write out how long it will take and be as specific as possible. Both short and long-term projections are crucial to your success. In the example I just used, the short-term projection would be seven years to accomplish your goal, but what if you take time off to work and save money? Maybe take two years off between undergraduate and graduate school, and now you are up to nine years to accomplish your goal. That would be a long-term projection. Both are essential so that you do not over or undershoot your time investment.

The other way to overcome this fear is to chunk it down. Instead of planning seven years into the future, which can seem overwhelming, chunk it down into smaller, bite-sized goals. With the example I stated, a first step would be just to graduate from high school. Once that is done, then you can plan undergraduate school. After that, you can assess graduate school. That way, you have three smaller goals, which are more attainable than one large goal, even though it is the same time commitment. A very important caveat would be to never lose sight of your main, overall objective! Smaller goals are only used to chop down your main goal, but we must always use this through the filter of your ultimate purpose and dream! Write out your long-term goal. Once you have it on paper, then you go through the process of chunking it down. With it chunked down, you will be able to overcome the fear of time that is holding you captive! With this fear gone from your mind, you will be unchained from the self-made prison keeping you from trying to set and achieve goals, especially long-term goals.

Rejection

The fear of rejection is one of the most pervasive of all the fears. Rejection is, quite possibly, the hardest fear to break through. This fear keeps people from even attempting to reach their dreams, and the crazy thing is this is not a fear that you have for yourself. The fear of rejection is the fear that some person, maybe a family member, or someone else completely, is going to reject your idea or goal or product you are tied to. This fear has nothing to do with your personality, your time, or the amount of work it will take to achieve success. Instead, this fear will keep you from even starting for fear of what other people will think of you or your idea. This fear is all about being "liked" or "accepted" by others.

I am not a psychologist. I am not going to attempt to wade through the minefield that is your past experience with approval issues, typically from a parent, coach, mentor, friend, etc. My goal is to help you see the problem and give you some solutions so you can start dealing with this issue. A simple phrase that has helped many people (me included) with this fear is "What is the worst thing that could happen?" Ask yourself this question when fear starts creeping up inside you. Then, take it to its most extreme end. Let's say your job requires you to sell vacuum cleaners. You are in front of the customer, about to make the sale. Ask yourself what is the worst thing that could happen? Let us pretend the person in front of you absolutely hates your sales pitch. Then what? He will throw you out of his house. Then what? He tells everyone he knows about you and they do not want to have you over to their house. Then what? You will lose all new customer referrals from that person. Then what? You will lose thousands of dollars. Then what? You will have to find new people to pitch your idea to. Then what? You have more work to do.

Now that we have the worst case scenario, look at your life. When you write down your scenario, it is easy to see that, for the most part, none of that will happen. Even if it does, you would still be fine! Why do we need to look at worst-case? It shows us two things: first, you can see how absurd the fear is that you carry, and second, even if the worst thing happened, you could still use it to help propel yourself forward!

After you look at the worst-case scenario, then look at the potential best case scenario. What if the person loves your sales pitch? Then what? You make the sale. Then what? He gives you a bunch of referrals that turns into 20 more sales. Then what? You become the most successful person in your trade. Then what? You will ACHIEVE YOUR GOAL! When you look at your fear from both perspectives, it becomes easy to see that the best choice is to go for the best case scenario. Chances are that even if the person tells you <u>NO</u>, the worst case scenario will not happen. That being said, you cannot achieve your best case scenario without going for it! As Nike says it, "just do it!"

One thing that has helped me with this same fear is statistical analysis. How many "no's" do I need to hear before I will get my first "yes"? Typically when I was first starting out, I would hear the word no over 100 times before I would ever get a yes. Talk about a lot of rejection! If I had looked at each no as an isolated event, it would have been easy to get disappointed. But, when you know through your own experience that you have to hear no 100 times before you get a yes, you can make a game of it. After that, hearing no becomes fuel for you, because it means you are one step closer to that desired yes!

Figure out your no number. Is it 50? 10? 1000? Whatever it is, this exercise will help you overcome the feeling of dread that comes from hearing that simple word. When you get to that point where you love hearing no, you can rest assured that you have completely conquered your fear of rejection! Not only will this help you get past hearing the word no, you will also succeed *faster*. The reason for this is because when you do not have the fear of rejection you will actually be excited to ask more people, to sell to more people, to interact with more prospective clients, because you will not be tied to the yes or the no. Your only motivation will be to sell yourself which will ensure massive success quickly. Is that what you are looking for? I thought so.

CHAPTER 2

DO YOU EVEN BELIEVE IN YOU?

"The man who does not value himself,
cannot value anything or anyone."

~ Ayn Rand

Fear is a major contributor to people who are not reaching

their optimal potential in life. Fear casts a long shadow that is

sometimes hard to get out from under. However, self-esteem is

not as easily conquered as fear! Self-esteem is another common

reason people have for not striving for success and abundance

and prosperity in life. By definition, self-esteem is simply the value

you put on yourself, or the value you put on your contributions to

society. Self-esteem has very little to do with other people. Low

self-esteem is the driving force that keeps people from stepping

out of the mundane, everyday life they currently have, into the

open where criticism could follow. People with low self-esteem

will usually try to blend in with the middle of the pack. It makes sense. If you have low self-esteem, you do not feel as if you have anything to contribute to the collective good, so you will try to stay in the middle of the pack, in order to avoid the limelight. So, how does a person develop his or her self-esteem? We know that self-esteem is not hereditary. Andrew Carnegie was one of the most successful business men in the history of the world, yet his father was not able to hold down a job for more than a couple of weeks. Henry Ford has a similar story. He came from a humble family farm to start one of the most successful automobile companies on the planet. Self-esteem is grown inside of each of us! It is not something handed down from our parents. It is cultivated over our lifetime. You have the ability to grow your self-esteem. Where you are currently is not where you need to end. It does not matter what anyone has said about you; what only matters is what you think about yourself.

That should be encouraging to you! Why? Because if you are lacking self-esteem, you simply have to develop more! The conceptual understanding of that is the easy part. The hard part is going through the steps necessary to develop self-esteem. I am going to give you some simple exercises you can use to increase your self-worth. Doing so is of utmost importance, because if you are unable to deliver your amazingly important skill to society, no one will ever be blessed by your talent! Your self-esteem issue is affecting everyone around you, most importantly, your family. You owe it to them to become the best version of yourself! Playing small because of a low self-esteem does not benefit anyone, you included. So how do we develop our self-esteem?

The first step to developing self-esteem is the realization that it does not matter what other people think about you! Reread that last sentence! Your self-worth is never predicated by other people's opinions of you. You are the only person who can decide what you are worth to society. It does not matter what your parents told you growing up. It does not matter what that one teacher told you in school. It does not even matter what your employer thinks of you. The only thing that matters is what you think of you! The first exercise in developing self-worth/esteem is to write down all (some, if too many to remember) the times someone said or did something that made you question your self-worth. With this list, what you need to do is find out if there are any common themes. In other words, are there things that keep surfacing? For example, does everything on your list make you feel like you are not good enough? Then you have negative self-feedback. We all have a consistent message that will negatively impact our self-esteem, unless we identify it and change the message. What is your negative message? Is it that you are too old? Is it that you do not have enough energy? Is it that you feel that you are not good enough? Whatever it is that keeps running through your mind, you need to identify it and change it to the opposite. An example would be "I am not good enough" changed to "I have the skills to be effective in all areas of my life." When you change the negative message to its opposite, positive message, it creates a feeling of self-worth and esteem that carries into your everyday activities. It changes the culture around you because you stop listening to what other people think of you, and you realize, fundamentally, that their opinion does not mean anything to your self-worth!

We just walked through the process of identifying your "limiting beliefs," those negative things that run constantly in your mind, and replacing them with your new "empowering beliefs." Every time you start thinking that negative, limiting belief, you instantly need to change the thought to your empowering belief! This changes the negative feedback into positive feedback, which instills further self-esteem, which spurs on further action.

The second step to developing your self-esteem, just like the first, is a realization. The first realization was that other people's opinion of you does not change your self-worth. Similarly, you need to realize that the only person's opinion that matters, other than your own, is God's opinion! Self-esteem is the confidence that you are fulfilling the purpose God has created for you. The

Bible tells us "Before I formed you in the womb I knew you, before you were born I set you apart; I appointed you as _____." (Jeremiah 1:5 – line added). God has appointed you to a specific role. He has set you apart from all the other creatures that he has created. You are His prized creation. He is so unbelievably proud and happy because you are His masterpiece! If God is proud of you and has nothing but great things to say about you, why would you listen to anyone else? Whose opinion is more important than God's? Why are you taking your self-esteem from other people and ignoring the confidence God has in you? You were set apart from birth to fulfill a calling that only you can do. God has created you and only you for that calling. Your job is to impact the people around you in a way that brings glory back to God. Sitting on the bleachers in the game of life is not what He had in mind. When you accept that you were created perfectly in His image, for a specific calling and purpose, it becomes easy to ignore what everyone else says or thinks about you!

In the Bible, the perfect example of someone short on self-esteem was the prophet Jeremiah. God explains to Jeremiah at the start of his prophet ministry that he was set apart from birth to perform the special task of being a prophet for God. God said, "Before you were born, I set you apart for a special work. I appointed you as a prophet to the nations." (Jer. 1:5b) Jeremiah's response shows us how he views himself. Jeremiah replies to God, "Then I said, 'But Lord God, I don't know how to speak. I am only a boy.'" (Jer. 1:6) This example perfectly displays low self-esteem. Jeremiah was told directly by God that he was specifically chosen to perform a job that only he could do, and what does Jeremiah say? I can't do it. He gives God reasons why God was wrong and why he (Jeremiah) would not be good for the gig. Can you picture God's face? God was probably thinking something along the lines of "I created you, warts and all, and I know EXACTLY what you can and cannot do!" Jeremiah was trying to sabotage himself before he even started. But, that is what low self-esteem will do. It will cripple you and keep you from experiencing all the wonders that God has for you--which He specifically created YOU to accomplish!

In what ways are you sabotaging yourself? How have you been trying to hide from the responsibilities that God has given you? What reasons (excuses) have you been using to back out of the job that God has for you? How are you going to change today so that you can stop denying your full potential and start living for your purpose? Jeremiah did not really have a choice in the matter. God told Jeremiah which way things were going to go. God said, "Jeremiah, get ready. Stand up and tell them everything I command you to say. Don't be afraid of the people, or I will give you good reason to be afraid of them." (Jer. 1:17) That got Jeremiah's attention! That reminds me of what my dad used to say to my brothers and me when we were fighting with each other, and one of us (usually my brothers) started crying. My dad would say "Stop crying or I'll give you something to cry about!" God is giving Jeremiah the same lecture. Stop being afraid and do what I have told you to do or I'll give you something to be afraid of! When my dad would say that to one of us, that was when all of us would quit, because none of us wanted "something to cry about." Can you imagine how much more intimidating that would be when God says it to you?

In what ways is God saying that to you right now? Has He been trying to get your attention for a while? Does He have something for you to do, that only you can do, that you were specifically created and gifted to accomplish? How can you start saying "yes" to God and "no" to the thoughts that tell you that you are not good enough, or skilled enough, or that you just are not the right person for the job?

Meditate on what God has gifted you with and the calling He placed in your heart. When you are living in that calling, you will not have issues with self-worth or self-esteem. You will be living out your purpose. No greater feeling in the world exists. No other method to increase your self-esteem even compares to when you are in line with God's calling for your life! So if you are suffering from a low self-esteem, that is an indicator that you need to reevaluate the direction your life is going, and see if God has been working on changing that direction to a more fulfilling one.

CHAPTER 3

HOW DO I DEVELOP CONFIDENCE?

"Look well into thyself; there is a source of strength which will always spring up if thou wilt always look."
~ Marcus Aurelius

Building from the last chapter, once a person's self-esteem is established, then we can develop the self-confidence needed to excel in life. Self-confidence is the measurement of someone's ability to believe in his or herself to accomplish goals and objectives. I am going to emphasize the crippling effects of low self-confidence and some proven methods for developing higher levels than you previously thought possible. If you are a person who does not believe in yourself, then buckle your seatbelt! This chapter is for you!

In order to build self-confidence, we first need to begin understanding it. Self-confidence is simply what we learned in the last chapter, self-esteem, plus experience. Once a person has value for him/herself, then the accumulation of experience and skills and training builds confidence in his/her abilities to succeed. Self-confident people have a certain swagger, a feeling that they could, and do, accomplish anything they put their mind to. This feeling is what creates the positive feedback loop that instills more confidence and leads to future successes! People with low self-confidence, on the other hand, start new responsibilities with a sense that they will not be able to succeed.

"Well, I failed before! Why should this time be any different?"

This self-defeating attitude is a killer to success in all avenues of life and business. I walked you through how to deal with that issue. For now, I want to show you the difference between self-confidence and prideful ego.

Kill the Ego

Undoubtedly, people will read this and think, "I know many people who have self-confidence, and they are horrible people to be around. They are always talking about themselves and always belittling other people. They think they are better than everyone else." Without question, as soon as you read this, someone will come to your mind who exemplifies those negative characteristics. Some people are afraid to develop confidence because they think they will somehow turn into the example I just mentioned. Fortunately, that person you first thought of does not portray high self-confidence, but instead high ego! People with high ego, for the most part, act egotistical because they are trying to cover up their really low self-esteem/self-confidence. They are acting confident, pretending to have it all together. When stripped bare, they are just as scared as anyone else; they just think they have to hide that fact. They try to replace their fear with ego, thinking that no one will notice the difference.

Ego is one of the ugliest faces you can ever show another person. Ego is all about self, but not in a confidence manner. Ego cares about self more than anyone else. Ego sacrifices others to keep itself elevated. Ego cares more about achieving status than it does achieving victory in its industry. Ego prefers to climb the corporate ladder by itself more than trying to help others achieve success. In fact, ego will sacrifice anyone else on the altar of self-fulfillment. Self-confidence, for the most part, is the opposite of ego. Self-confidence wants to win, but not at the expense of others. Ego says, "I am the best!" Self-confidence says, "Our team is the best!" Ego says, "I will just have to do it myself." Self-confidence as, "I have to spend more time training, so we all can do it." Ego says, "I deserve this or that." Self-confidence says, "I will be rewarded when the time is right."

Can you see the difference? Go through and analyze yourself. Where do you stand? Do you lean more one way or the other? Do you have too much ego? In what ways does your ego show itself? Write it down! This next part will be the hardest exercise for you to do if you have too much ego. Pick 3 to 5 people who are very close to you, people who will tell you the truth, even if it hurts your feelings. Ask them to rate you, on a scale of 0 – 10, 10 being the most obnoxious, egotistical maniac on the planet, and 0 being Mother Theresa. Take all the ratings and average them out, then add 2! Whatever number you get after you add the 2 is the number that you would get rated by people who do not love you! This will either be a good exercise for you, showing you how pious you are, or a painful exercise, showing who you really care about most in life...yourself! No matter what it tells you, use it to grow and improve. One thing to keep in mind, when doing this exercise, is that the higher your ego, the harder it is going to be to accept the reality of the results. People with high egos typically cannot accept negative critiquing, and will go as far as to deny the truth in order to be right. Hopefully that is not you, but if it is, that is okay. If you find yourself vehemently denying or pushing back against the feedback of people who care about you most in this world, then that is an indication that your ego is too high! Now that you realize this about yourself, YOU HAVE TO CHANGE! If you want to grow and succeed and change the world, you have to start with yourself!

Build Your Confidence

Assuming you are not the ego-driven person, but instead, like the majority of people, one who lacks self-confidence, what can you do to build yourself up? The first step, just like in the last chapter, is finding the self-defeating thought patterns that consistently flood your mind. These patterns are the negative influence that causes doubt and self-disbelief. The three most common self-defeating thought patterns listed below:

1) The "all or nothing" thought.
2) Accepting emotional responses as truth.
3) Difficulty accepting compliments from others.

To better understand these three patterns, let's dissect them in order for you to obtain a clear, objective mindset shift (paradigm shift) away from self-defeating into self-confidence!

1) The "all or nothing"

Many people with low self-confidence get trapped by this pervasive mindset. If I do not do it perfectly the first time I try, then I am a complete failure, worthy of scorn and criticism. Not only is this incredibly toxic, it is also unrealistic. Can you see why? Everything you do in the future will have the expectation of past failures looming over it. Every future endeavor will be met with failure at some level because of this negative, self-defeating thought process. The saddest part of this is that very few things in life are all or nothing! There can be victories, however small, in everything! But, a person with this worldview will not be able to see those victories. The easiest way to overcome this self-defeating mindset is to create a victory wall or victory book.

What is a victory wall? A victory wall is a literally a billboard that contains all your past victories. Whether in sports, high school classes, social events, friends, work, church, etc., it is a monument to all the positive accomplishments you have achieved in your life! You take images of past victories, cut them out (newspaper clippings, photos, etc.,) and place them on this billboard. This shows and reminds you that there are positives in everything. This becomes a visual representation of past victories, which affirms us and builds us up in order to have more confidence in future events or goals. What does your victory wall look like? Take however much time you need to craft and create your own victory wall. Use pictures, drawings if you are creative, words, etc. The more vivid you can make your wall, the more positive emotions it will bring you, which will spur you on to more victory for your next project! Positive emotions are the driving force towards further victory in life. That emotion is what motivates you to continue learning, to continue striving forward, and to continue reaching for your goals, even in the event of failures. Failures are going to happen; they are inevitable. But what is not inevitable, is whether or not you are going to rise to the occasion after you fail. Charles Kettering said, "The only time you can't afford to fail is the last time you try." How many times you fall in life is not what matters most, but how many times you get back up. The emotions created from your victory wall are what help you get back up after you fall.

2) Accepting emotional responses as truth

People of low self-confidence have a very hard time with this self-defeating thought. Emotions are designed to help us cope with situations or circumstances. An event happens, and we have an emotional response to that event. Emotions are supposed to come as a response mechanism and leave when the event is over. It normally happens that way. What is not normal, however, is when we extrapolate that emotional feeling as a truth about us. We have experiences that generate these emotional feelings all the time. I will give you some examples of this.

"I look in the mirror and feel ugly, so others see me that way, too."

"I did poorly on this assignment and feel stupid, so I must not be very smart."

"I was rejected by someone I liked and now I feel unloved, so I will never be loved by anyone."

The hardest part about this self-defeating thought is that we are the ones creating it. Likely it is based on something said to you by a person of authority in your life (parent, teacher, etc.), but you are the one holding onto it. Furthermore, every time you feel that emotion, it will negatively destruct all the positivity in your life. This causes emotional bankruptcy and spurs on the perpetual feeling of not being good enough.

The only way to overcome emotions and feelings is with other emotions and feelings. Every time an emotionally negative feeling creeps in, you need to have its opposite ready to be expressed. You have a feeling of sadness; replace it with a thought that makes you overwhelmingly happy (like the birth of a child, wedding day, etc.). If you start feeling like you are inadequate, or not good enough, replace it with a thought of the most successful you have ever been (winning a championship, earning the promotion, acing a test, completing a project, etc.). Whenever you have a negative emotion rear its ugly head, you need to be ready with its opposite positive emotion! This, in effect, has a cancelling affect on the negative emotion and leaves you feeling happy about yourself. Replacing a negative feeling with a positive feeling builds self-confidence, instead of tearing down your self-confidence!

3) Difficulty accepting compliments from others

If this self-defeating thought is the one that plagues your subconscious mind, you can take a breath of relief. Overcoming this difficulty is quite possibly the easiest one to do. I am in no way trying to minimize the damaging effect this can have on self-confidence. I only want you to realize that you can change this thought process easily, if you want to badly enough!

The most effective way to start accepting compliments from others is to start accepting them from you. How often do you give yourself compliments? More than likely, not enough! This needs to be a daily process, where first thing in the morning you find five things to compliment about yourself. For many women (guys too), the first thing they say when looking in the mirror is "I do not like how I look." The first thought is negative. How can you expect to receive compliments from others when you cannot give praise to yourself? Other people are not going to give you the intrinsic value you are withholding from yourself! Start your day off with positive compliments to yourself and watch how much easier it will become to receive them from others, which will crank up the self-confidence you have in yourself!

In this chapter we have discussed multiple issues that affect self-confidence. We saw how the ego can and does reflect poorly on your personality, and that it is a sign of low self-confidence. I gave you steps to check your ego level with five people you trust and respect. In this way, you can start processing your ego level and start replacing it with true self-confidence.

Next, we walked through the three most common self-defeating thoughts that cripple our self-confidence. For each one, I gave simple exercises to overcome them, which will start building your inner strength to bolster your confidence levels. Take what you have learned and start applying it in your life

RIGHT NOW! These principles will pull you out of the rut you are chained to by low self-confidence. You make these simple changes and your self-confidence should go up, people will start seeing you as the leader you are, and most importantly, you will respect yourself!

CHAPTER 4

REGRET IS A PROGRESSIVE CANCER

"I'd rather regret the things I've done than regret the things I haven't done."

~ Lucille Ball

When learning how to ride a bike, most of us were taught with training wheels. Training wheels were used to allow us to practice, but without the danger of falling down and hurting ourselves. Riding a bike is a good example of how regret and low self-confidence work together to hold you back in life. Low self-confidence keeps you from transitioning away from the training wheels of life and into the real world. Regret keeps reminding you what happened when you eventually decided to transition into self-confidence. Do you remember what happened when you first took off the training wheels? If you were like me, you crashed multiple times! Regret then tells you that you should have stayed within the comfort of the training wheels, which keeps you from moving on to bigger and better things in life. One of the fastest ways to stifle growth in life, within families, between spouses, or in business is through regret. What is regret? How does it impede progress through life? What can we do to move past regret? These are all questions I get when on the topic of regret.

So what is regret? The definition of regret according to Merriam-Webster is "a feeling of sadness or disappointment about something that you did or did not do." I would rephrase that to say it is remembering something (event, person, or place) with the feeling of loss or sorrow. Another way to put it is a feeling of disappointment about something you wish could be different. So basically regret is reliving something from your past (person, interaction, circumstance) with the feeling of disappointment because if you could do it over, you would do it differently. Can you see how toxic that thought process is to future growth? You are unable to grow, adapt, change, and move on to better things because you are stuck in the past! Do you know what part in this is the most frustrating? No matter how badly you want to change what happened, you cannot do anything about it!

The scary truth about regret is that if you do not address it, you are doomed to repeat the past mistake (or perceived mistake). So how do you move past the regret that is causing you to live life looking backwards? The mechanism for moving on is pretty straightforward. First, you need to identify exactly what you regret. Write it out. What happened? How did you respond/react? What was said or done to cause the feeling of regret? What has transpired in the wake of this event? How has that shaped your expectations of the future? Put it all out on paper (or blog, if that is your flavor).

Now you can see the whole picture; you next need to analyze the situation. Was there something you could have done differently to avoid what happened? What caused it to happen in the first place? What role did you play? How would you have stopped it from happening, if you could change it? Was there anything you could have done? Write down on paper specific answers to these questions. This will paint a different picture because you can see it from all angles. Maybe there was something you could have done differently to change the outcome. More than likely though, there was nothing you could have done that would have had the slightest impact on the outcome. You need to take a realistic, third-party look at the scenario and create a sense of forgiveness for yourself, because no matter which way you answer the questions, it is already done, and nothing will change that! You cannot rewrite the past, only learn from it. Do not let past events dictate your future happiness!

One of the most well-known stories of regret comes from the Book of "John" in the *Bible*. The 12 apostles and Jesus are sitting together, having their "Last Supper." Jesus is telling them about what is to come, the crucifixion, and about his coming back from the grave three days later. He also tells the apostles how he will only be with them for a short while longer, and where he goes, they cannot follow. In typical Peter fashion, (Peter was always the first to speak, usually very brazenly, and always making proclamations that were full of ego and pride) he says, "Lord, why can't I follow you? I am ready to die for you!" (John 13:37) Can you see what I mean about brazen? Jesus tells them they cannot follow, and Peter basically says, "Nope, you are wrong; I am coming with you." Can you picture the look that Jesus is giving Peter at this point? I can only imagine watching Jesus sigh, look down, then look Peter straight in the eyes to tell him the next part. "Jesus answered, 'Are you ready to die for me? I tell you the truth, before the rooster crows, you will say three times that you don't know me.'" (John 13:38) Peter would deny Jesus three times before the night was over.

After Jesus was taken by the Roman guards, Peter and

John followed behind to see what was going to happen. If you want to read about Peter's denials in the Bible, you can read it in John 13: 15-27. Peter was asked three different times if he was with Jesus (one of his followers) and Peter denied knowing Jesus all three times. After Peter's third denial, the rooster crowed, reminding Peter what Jesus had told him earlier that night at the Last Supper. Peter was so upset and angry with himself that he ran off crying. (Luke 22:62)

We know what happened next. Jesus was crucified, and the apostles were not sure what to do next. Peter felt like he lost his purpose, having betrayed his Lord. Without knowing what else to do, Peter decides that it is time to go back to his old life (most of the apostles were fisherman before Jesus came around). Has that ever happened to you? You felt like you were so close to achieving your dream, reaching your goal, accomplishing your mission, and then splat, you fell on your face! What do you do then? For most people, Peter included, you go back to the old life. You leave behind the new and go back to the old, mundane life you were living before you took the leap of faith and stepped outside of your comfort zone to try something new. So often I hear people tell me how they tried to reach their dream, only to have something happen to stop them. What do you do when you meet adversity? The answer to that question is what determines successes in life from continued failures. What is more, the people who do quit when it gets tough are the same people who need to overcome regret later on in life! I would be hard pressed to find a more perfect example of what causes regret. So, how does Peter come out of his cycle of regret to become one of the greatest apostles of all time?

While the apostles were fishing, Jesus (reincarnated) comes to them and yells from the shore, "Friends, did you catch any fish?" (John 21:5). I actually picture Jesus laughing when he is saying this to the apostles, because he knew full well that they hadn't caught any fish! I love Jesus' sense of humor in this situation. The apostles answer with a no, and Jesus tells them to throw their net over the right side of the boat and they will catch some fish. They do this and catch so many fish that the net starts to break. The apostles recognize Jesus and rush to shore to see him. They took some of their fish and then cooked them for lunch.

After eating, Jesus asks Peter three times if he loves him. Peter replied all three times that he does love Jesus. When you read this, you can almost hear Peter getting annoyed with Jesus. The third time Peter replies with "Lord, you know everything; you know that I love you!" (John 21:17b). Why do you suppose Jesus asked Peter three times if he loved him? I do not pretend to know everything that God does, but it would seem that Jesus was asking him once for each time that Peter denied him. Jesus was helping Peter forgive himself! Jesus understood regret, knew that regret had caused Peter to completely leave the ministry after Jesus died, and Jesus needed to reenlist him. Peter needed to forgive himself; that was the only way for Peter to overcome his regret. Jesus is showing Peter that even though Peter made a mistake, God still knows Peter's heart and that he loves Jesus more than anything. Jesus already knew this; he was allowing Peter to know he knew that! The only person who was condemning Peter was Peter! Jesus was teaching Peter how to forgive himself, and in the process, heal himself of his regret. In what areas do you need to forgive yourself? Where do you need to have a realistic talk with yourself (or Jesus) to have forgiveness and freedom from regret?

What Is The Truth In This Situation?

"What is the truth in this situation?" is quite possibly the best question you can ask yourself in all situations where you feel things did not go your way. This question helps pull out the lesson that you needed to learn. It leaves behind all the "what if's" and gleams out the gems that will help propel you forward in life. Unfortunately, too many people pull a past event into present circumstances. This ensures you will continue to make the same mistakes over and over again. What is worse than that? When you take past events and project them into future scenarios, which is devastating to growth, you become stagnant from all the inactivity. Now, not only is the regret playing your mind, but you have created an event in the future which has not yet happened. That leads to fear. So now you have two things to overcome! These two things cause paralysis, which keeps you in the mistake/fear cycle. The mistake/fear cycle is hard to leave. You make the mistake, causing regret. Regret allows the fear to creep in your head. Fear keeps you from trying anything new to change your circumstance because of the memories of those past failures. Your past failures loom over you, crippling future growth! Can you see how destructive this can be? Peter could not let go of his regret. He kept playing it over and over in his mind. One event (in the past) pushed him to make the decision to go back to fishing (affecting his present circumstances) and quit ministry altogether (future events altered and affected by past regret). In what ways are you doing this exact same thing? How have you taken something from your past and pulled it into your present, then projected it into your future? You HAVE to forgive yourself! You will never be free of the event (regret) if you do not let it go! How do you let it go? How do you overcome?

The way through regret is to keep past events where they

belong—in the past! Stop allowing past regrets to shape your future outcomes. The way to do that is by realizing what was gained by experience. Too many of us only see mistakes. Stop and redefine the experience. In which ways am I better off for having gone through that experience? Write them down. See the past for what it is—a useful tool for development and personal growth!

It will take some time to learn how to do this effectively. Life is a journey on the path to self-improvement, not a race. What have your past regrets been trying to tell you all along? What lesson is there, waiting for you to learn from it? These truths will give you the push you need to break through regrets. Peter, if you remember, ended up being a super apostle and one of the most influential people on the planet at that time. However, if he would not have forgiven himself, he would have stayed a fisherman, and no one would have written anything about him! Time for you to throw the fishing pole away and step into the person you are called to be. Let the regret go, and watch your life take off! You can accomplish this! You only have to forgive yourself!

I am reminded of a patient of mine who suffered from regret. Stephanie was a normal young woman who struggled letting go of past events. She could not forgive herself for past failures. Specifically, she struggled with feelings of not meeting the expectations of the people she cared about. In her attempt to be perfect for others (unrealistic), she continued to be plagued with regret for falling short of where she wanted to be. As a friend of mine puts it, she is a recovering perfectionist! With Stephanie, I simply helped her see how no one is really expecting her to be perfect, so why should she expect herself to be perfect? The two of us have had multiple discussions on this topic, because this is not something that can be "fixed" (for lack of a better word) with one discussion. She is a work in progress and is letting some of the regret fall away. Powerful things happen when you can just forgive yourself and let it go! Keep working on it! You can overcome!

In this chapter we have looked at a few different ways in order to overcome past regrets. The best tool to utilize is the saying "What is the truth in this situation?" By utilizing this sentence, you gain a new perspective over your situation, or past circumstances, that you did not have before. This perspective allows you to see that even though the outcome was not favorable, it was not as bad as you originally accepted it to be. This will help you get over the past event that has been plaguing your mind for years! Now that you know this, who can you help? Many people in your sphere of influence are suffering with this same problem. You could be the answer! This simple sentence "What is the truth in this situation?" could change a lot of lives. You could change a lot of lives! Share this information and help others!

CHAPTER 5

SKILLS CAN BE ACHIEVED THROUGH TRAINING

"Talent is cheaper than table salt. What separates the talented individual from the successful one is a lot of hard work."
~ Stephen King

The last thing that holds a person back, and the last thing we will discuss in part one of this book is what to do if you do not have the skills, talents, or abilities necessary to move to the next level in your organization or in your life. We will briefly discuss the mindset that is pervasive with this line of thinking. Also, we will walk through simple steps to overcome this thought process.

First and foremost, when it comes to diagnosing your problem, you have to assess whether this is, in fact, the truth-- meaning you do have insufficiencies in your life or is this just how you perceive the situation? What do I mean by this? Do you need to improve your skill and cultivate your talent, or is it all in your head and you are indeed good enough? Too many people look in the mirror and feel less than or a sense of disappointment. They feel they are not as good as so-and-so. They cannot be as good as someone else (you know who that person is in your life--the one you put on a pedestal). What is the truth of the situation? Do you need additional work? Is there someone else with more skill than you?

This reminds me of Moses in the Old Testament. God wanted Moses to lead his people (the Israelites) out of slavery and into the Promised Land. The way that God spoke to Moses was through a burning bush. "So now I am sending you to the king of Egypt. Go! Bring my people, the Israelites, out of Egypt!" (Exodus 3:10) God is giving Moses a direct command. God tells Moses that he has been chosen to do this, and he needs to do this right away. Moses was not as confident as God, however, and started making excuses for his lack of talent and skills. "But Moses said to God, 'I am not a great man! How can I go to the king and lead the Israelites out of Egypt?'" Moses is discrediting himself in front of God. He is trying to convince God that he is not the right man for the job. Go and read Exodus chapters three and four to get the full story. What amazes me is how we tell ourselves we are not good enough for a certain job, or how we do not have a certain skill to be effective at something. We are lying to ourselves so that we will not have to step out of our comfort zone. Moses is telling God this, not because he is deliberately trying to be difficult, but because he desperately wants to continue working on his father-in-law's farm. The work is easy! He does the same thing each and every day. A mundane life holds a sense of simplicity. In that line of work (shepherd), he never has to step outside of himself and get uncomfortable! God is not convinced, however!

God gives Moses the ability to perform not one, not two, but THREE miracles in order to show the Israelites he was sent from God. Even after that, Moses STILL tries to tell God he is not the right person for the job. "But Moses said to the Lord, 'Please Lord, I have never been a skilled speaker. Even now, after talking to you, I cannot speak well. I speak slowly and can't find the best words'" (Exodus 4:10). After everything that God has told him, Moses still does not believe himself capable of performing the duties God has called him to do. Isn't that like us? Even when divine intervention would have us do a certain job or calling or mission, we make all kinds of excuses in order to discredit ourselves. We make all these assertions that we would not be able to succeed, long before we even try. We quit before we even start! Moses was trying that here, with God. Fortunately, God was having none of it! "Then the Lord said to him, 'Who made a person's mouth? And who makes someone deaf or not able to speak? Or who gives a person sight or blindness? It is I, the Lord. Now Go! I will help you speak, and I will teach you what to say'" (Exodus 4:11, 12). You would think that would be the end of the discussion. Moses at this point has been given multiple miracles to perform, been told that God will literally put all the words in his mouth and speak for him, what else is there to say? Moses, not to be outdone, pleads one more time with God. "But Moses said, 'Please, Lord, send someone else'" (Exodus 4:13). Does this sound familiar? Even with all the odds stacked in our favor, just like Moses, we still try to find ways out of a situation! God, however, has had enough of Moses' excuses. Now, He is mad! "The Lord became angry with Moses and said, 'Your brother Aaron, from the family of Levi, is a skilled speaker. He is already coming to meet you, and he will be happy when he sees you. You will speak to Aaron and tell him what to say. I will help both of you to speak and will teach you what to do. Aaron will speak to the people for you. You will tell him what God says, and he will speak for you. Take your walking stick with you, and use it to do the miracles'" (Exodus 4:14-17).

I love the finality of that last sentence. God is not allowing any more discussion. He tells Moses "You will," meaning there is no more debating about whether or not Moses will be doing this job. The best part of this story is how God was moving Moses' brother Aaron into the story, even before Moses complained about his poor speaking skills. God has placed the right people in our lives to help us accomplish our calling and mission. He tells Moses to get moving and reassures him that He will be right there to help with the completion! God's reassurance brings me comfort. God is there--ready to help me out, especially when I do not have the correct skills developed yet. In many ways, God wants you to start moving BEFORE you have the skills, because He gets the credit for the victory.

Who has God put in your life to help you achieve your dreams? Is there someone in your organization who could help you overcome your limited skill or talent? I am guessing someone at your place of employment has gone through what you are going through right now. Could you ask them for help? I am sure they would be willing to help you develop, because they remember being in your place before someone helped them! Who is that person? How do you find out who it is that you need to ask?

First, find out who is the absolute best at your position. Second, figure out what they did to get to the position. With the exception of nepotism, that person gained favor and respect by working hard in training to be the best! If that person did it, so can you! What did they do to get there? How long did it take them to master the position? What were the obstacles on the climb to the top? How can you avoid the same pitfalls? Asking these questions of that person will give you the power of understanding what it will take to elevate yourself past the limitations and barriers holding you back. Most every person who has achieved success had to start where you currently are to get to where they are now! You can take encouragement from that because he/she figured out what to do and so can you. Ask that person (the one who has gone through the challenges you are going through) these questions! Chances are he/she will love to help you get better because when his employees improve, productivity will improve, which will improve the bottom line of the office, which will then reflect positively, further elevating that person to the next level. Leadership is also characterized by that type of action. To be a leader is to help others become better than you currently are, so as to motivate others to improve the bottom line!

When you are meeting with this person who is currently above you, ask those questions. Also, ask if you could be mentored through the process of growth. This moves me into the next step of growth, which is coaching.

Everyone needs a coach! The best athletes in the world have coaches. Tiger Woods, albeit he is not a good role model off the golf course, is a perfect example of getting coaching. He is arguably the best golfer in the history of the sport. You would not, therefore, be surprised to find out he has a coach for every aspect of golf. He has a coach for his driver (the first club a golfer hits), a coach for his middle irons, a coach for his chipping, and a coach for his putting. What makes him the best is he doesn't think he knows it all, but finds and surrounds himself with people who do! Find the expert in your field and ask him/her to mentor you. If you have to pay them for what they know, DO IT! This will be the best investment for your resources when you invest in yourself! Find a great coach who will push you to be a better person every day.

The last step I will discuss in this chapter is training. Do you really want to get better, improve your skills, improve your positive outcomes, get the raise, make the promotion; and elevate yourself? If you said yes, then your next step is training. You have to hone your craft to increase your ability for growth.

In any service industry, a person does not get paid for service rendered. He/she gets paid for the amount of training done before the service was provided! Have you ever thought about how two companies can provide the same service; one charges $1000 for their service and the other charges only $100 for their service? The service provided is the exact same! How can one company charge 10 times more than what the competition charges? How is it that the company charging 10 times more has more business than its cheaper counterpart? The reason why is because people will pay more for better service provided by someone with more skill in that sector! What does that mean for you? The harder you self-train at your skill or craft, the better you get, the more your customers will value your service, the more they will *want* to pay you for that service! You do not charge more to make more money. You charge more because you are better! Own that fact, and it will change your life!!

      The best example I have to show you what I mean is in my own experience. When I first started taking patients in to my practice, I did not have much value for my skill set, and because of that, I did not charge much for my service. I continuously grew my practice, and because of that, I was forced to train more to keep improving to help more people. With the increased training, my skills grew exponentially. It took me years to realize how little I was charging for the service I was providing. It started with a slight increase (5%) in billing. People kept paying me, so I increased again to meet demand (10%). My practice continued to grow, and because of my commitment to training, so did my skill set! The difference in value from when I first started practicing to today is much higher! The only thing that changed was the amount of training I had to do to meet the expectations of my clientele. With the increased training comes an increase in value for what you do. Your value increase is what allows you to take your life to the next level!

In this chapter we walked through the four main areas where skill, talent, and ability can hold you back and what you can do to overcome these obstacles. We discussed how most of these obstacles are in your own mind. We went over self-evaluation and how we constantly need to be evaluating our training and skills. Moses showed us that sometimes, even when we feel as though we are not good enough, we need to just move, and God will help us along the way! As we saw with Moses, his excuses were not even valid. He was the perfect person for the job; he just did not realize it! How about you? Are you going to believe the lies you are telling yourself?
Are you really not good enough, or are you, in fact, the perfect person for the job?

We talked about finding a mentor to help you through the transitions of growth in your career. We discussed finding a coach, or multiple coaches, to help you develop yourself into the person necessary for improvement. Lastly, we covered the importance of training. The only way someone will ever be better than you is if they train harder than you. Just do not let them!

When it comes right down to it, hard work and constant training is something within your power to launch your career to wherever you want to go! With these steps, you are now ready to move on to the next part of this book, which is "Cultivating Your Character."

PART 2

CULTIVATING YOUR CHARACTER

CHAPTER 6

DISCIPLINE YOURSELF!

"Success isn't measured by money or power or social rank.
Success is measured by your discipline and inner peace."
~ Mike Ditka

The first part of this book was all about finding out and examining what issue or multiple issues are holding you back. You were given simple exercises that will help you overcome these limitations. I fully recognize that some problems will take longer to conquer than one exercise--which is why you need repetition! Some of these exercises will have to be redone over and over again until you have actually overcome whatever is holding you back.

Now that you are on your way to defeating your self-limiting mindset, we need to develop the character of a winner. The next three chapters are dedicated to "Cultivating Your Character."

This chapter specifically is about the discipline it takes—and how to create the discipline needed—to advance yourself to the next levels in life, business, and anywhere else you want to go.

The biggest pitfall to discipline is time-wasting. One of the most common excuses I hear as to why something could not or will not get done is "I do not have enough time for that." This is by far the most frustrating excuse I hear! Why does this excuse bother me so much? The answer is simple. We were all given the same amount of time in a day! We all have 24 hours. The difference between successful people who get stuff done and those people who constantly make excuses for not getting things done is time appropriation! Massively successful people get things done by setting aside time each day for their most important tasks. They do not have any more time than anyone else; they just use it better!

Step one in time appropriation (time management/mapping) is to plan out your day. Successful people use time mapping to manage and allocate their time resourcefully. A quote that has always stuck with me is "Either you can spend your time, or someone else will spend it for you." Either you plan out your time utilization or it will be wasted by others (or yourself) doing stuff that will not help you get past your current situation or achieve your goal.

The second step is to figure out your order of importance. As one of my mentors, Dr. Charles Majors says, "Which 3 to 5 things have to get done today before I go to sleep?" Those 3 to 5 things are your top priorities of importance and must get done at the expense of your sleep. Just imagine, how much better would your life, your work, your family, your marriage, etc., be if you made sure to get your top 3 to 5 things done each and every day? Picture it, how much faster your climb to the top would be if you always got your projects done on time, with extra time to work on other things? It would be a tremendous benefit for your workload and also a great stress relief! The greatest cause of stress at work is the feeling that you have more to do than time to do it. The stress would be gone if you knew exactly where your time is being spent! Pick your top 3 to 5 things that are "must do's." Prioritize every other activity after your "must do's" are completed. This will ensure that your top priorities get done first, and your secondary priorities come after.

I will give you two examples of this in action. The first example is what my "must do's" look like, and if I get them done, what a "could do" looks like. The second example is what my wife's list might look like in any given day, being that she is a stay-at-home mom with a part time job as an online teacher at a college.

With my day, 3 must do's might be:

1. Get notes done on patient visits to be submitted to insurance.
2. Train staff members on new procedures in the office.
3. Spend 30 minutes writing my new book.

After these are accomplished, I would be able to move on to could do's, which might be:

1. Mow the lawn.

2. Take my son to the park.

3. Do a blog post.

4. Read a new book.

5. Enjoy a cup of coffee.

You get the point? After I complete my list of must do's, I am able to do the things I would like to do (could do's.) Here is a sample of what my wife Mikala's list might look like:

1. Make sure my son has food to eat, i.e. make breakfast, lunch, and dinner.
2. When my son takes his nap, go online and upload grading from last exam.

3. During that same nap, create a new homework assignment for her students to do.

4. Plan activities for her and my son to do during the day that are fun and engaging so he continues to be actively learning while having fun (semi home-schooling.)

When she gets all of that done, then she can move on to her could do list, which sometimes is as simple as taking a bath or talking on the phone with a friend.

This should be a freeing activity for you to complete. Your time map will give you the leverage you need to start accomplishing all the tasks you need to get done. Some people will undoubtedly think this is too rigid and too structured for them. Those same people probably think time-mapping creates robots that use all their time doing tasks with no flexibility for spontaneity. Unfortunately, those are the same people who complain that they do not have enough time in a day to complete all their responsibilities. It goes hand-in-hand. The truth of the situation is a planned out time map, will allow you the intentionally mapped out free time. That way you get time for yourself. Do you want to know the best part about creating an accurate time map? It allows you MORE free time, while still getting your responsibilities done! You just need a change of mindset about it. The vast majority of successful people on the planet use a very specific time map! If they do it, I suggest you give it a try!

Orrin Woodward, in his best-selling book *Resolved 13 Resolutions for Life,* explains this process as PDCA; Plan, Do, Check, Adjust. In his system, the first step is PLAN! Your time map is your PLAN. Without it, you are flowing through your day hoping you are being efficient and effective. With a time map, you can rest assured that you are going to get done exactly what you set out to accomplish!

Step three in disciplining yourself is getting up early. I probably just lost half of you reading this book. You are thinking, "I can identify my fears, I can improve my self-esteem and self-confidence, I can let go of my past regrets, I can even work on my skills, talents and ability, and I will go far enough to set a time map, but come on, now I have to lose sleep by getting up early?" Do you have to get up early? YES! Do you have to lose sleep? NO! Most people do not have problems getting up early; they have a problem going to bed on time. For the successful business person (or anyone, really), nothing good happens past 10:00 PM. Therefore, why are you still awake? The only acceptable answer to that question is that you were reading this book. To that I say, read on! All joking aside, how much different would your day be if you got up at 6:00 AM, had time to exercise quickly, read your Bible, eat a good breakfast, shower, get to work early, and even check two things off your list before anyone else even got there? How much better would you feel about your day? Do you think your boss would notice that? You better believe it!

I can give you an example of how this works in the real world. One of my first jobs after college was in a courthouse looking at old documents. As a rule, I made sure that I was always early for work. I wasn't over-the-top with when I showed up for work; I just made sure that I was one of the (if not the) first ones there. If the courthouse opened at 8:00am, I made sure to be standing outside the door at 7:45am so I could be the first one there. With that industry, it is "first come, first served" in the vault where all the documents are kept. If you were not one of the first four people in line, you would not be able to set up your workstation inside the vault, which is where all the documents are kept. Instead, you would be put in the hallway, which is anywhere from 20 feet to 200 feet away from the documents! Some people did not care how far their workstation was from the documents, because they did not care *how much* work they accomplished each day, knowing there would be more tomorrow. I made it a personal challenge to get as much done each day as I could, thereby necessitating I be in the vault closest to the documents so that I did not need to walk back and forth between looking at documents. Why this helped me was when worked slowed down after a couple of years and the company had to let people go (fire them) I was one of the people who kept his job! The reason this is important is because hard work and planning pays off in the long run! Had I not gotten up early and started my day properly, I would not have gotten to the courthouse earlier than everyone else, which would have meant I would have been in the hallway, which would have meant I would have not gotten as much work done as someone else, which would have meant I would have been on the chopping block when the firing started! Luck favors the prepared.

Unfortunately, a common start to the work-day goes something like this. By the time someone actually gets out of bed, they have hit the snooze button five times, so instead of 6:00 AM, it is now 10 to 7:00 AM, and they have to be at work at 8:00 AM. Now they decide there isn't enough time to work out and they skip it. Instead, they jump in the shower and stay in for 30 minutes, trying to wake up. Now, by the time they are dressed, there is only 20 minutes left to get to work and clock in. With that timeline, not enough time is left to eat something healthy, so a doughnut from the gas station will have to do (oh, and a large coffee to go). They speed 20 miles over the speed limit, which causes incredible stress, just to get to work on time, and they pull a Dale Earnhardt power slide into their parking spot and sprint up the rest of the way to get their desk (so I guess they got their workout after all). Now they are stressed to the max and not at all mentally prepared for the challenges that today will bring!

The saddest part about the second scenario that I just explained is that these people are the ones who would say they do not have enough time to get their work done! These people would also be the first ones to argue that you do not need to be structured and rigid with a time map, because it takes away from the day's flexibility! Can you see the problem with that?

Now, instead of going to bed at midnight and starting the snooze button ritual because they are exhausted from lack of sleep, why not go to sleep at 10:00 PM? I would urge them to use their time map so they could get to bed earlier! They will get their full eight hours of uninterrupted (no snooze button) sleep, and they will still be able to jump out of bed at 6:00 AM! There is a choice to make here, but I think it is a pretty easy one!

In this chapter, we learned how to appropriate your time

with a time map. We also went over finding your top 3 to 5 things that <u>HAVE</u> to get done before you go to sleep at night. Lastly, we looked at how different your day could be if you used a time map, and consequently, went to bed earlier. With all of these tools in place, you are now ready for the next level of growth, which is the process of setting the goals that you want to achieve in life.

CHAPTER 7

DO YOU HAVE A GOAL?

*"If you don't know where you are going,
you'll end up someplace else."*

~ Yogi Berra

The next step to "Cultivating Your Character" is setting a goal. Many people ask at this point "Why set goals at all? I will just work really hard and everything will work out for the best!" To speak to that mindset, yes, if you work hard, you will most definitely be successful at some level. The problem I see with this mindset, however, is how are you measuring your success? What are the metrics (measurements) you are using? How are you today compared to where you were last month? Last year? Five years ago? If you do not have a goal(s), how are you consistently monitoring progress? Sure, work hard and be successful, but what if you are way short of where you could be and should be at this point in your life? What if, by setting goals, you can avoid some major pitfalls that affect others in your industry (or workplace)? Or, instead of taking ten years to achieve success, what if you could do it in eight? Or five? Or one? Best of all, you are the one setting the goal! You can push yourself as hard or soft as you want to be pushed! But, if you do not have goals, how do you know how hard you need to be pushed? How many hours need to be worked to achieve your desired level of success? How many deals need to be made? How many meetings need to be set up? If you do not have goals, you are walking (or pushing) upstream against the current, when you could just turn around and go with the current. Work smarter, get more done in less time, have more success, enjoy life more, and have more fun while doing it. The choice is yours, and if you are reading this book, then I think I know which choice you will make!

Goal Setting 101

All goals, whether made by the CEO of a Fortune 500 company or by some high school athlete, have a few things in common. All goals have to be <u>specific</u>, <u>measurable</u>, <u>achievable</u>, <u>relevant</u>, and <u>time-bound</u>. This process of goal-setting is called SMART. SMART goals have been around for decades. SMART goals first appeared in a November, 1981 issue of *Management Review* (vol. 70, issue 11.) SMART goals have all the components to ensure you achieve success. By following the steps I will lay out, you will have your greatest chance to achieve your goals. Breaking down these steps is the key to starting your path to success.

To clarify each point in the SMART goals process, I will use an example of a truck driver and his route. His job is to deliver goods from one place to another. Also, he needs to do it as quickly as possible. Lastly, he needs to be safe while delivering the merchandise (I know there are more steps than this, but for the sake of clarity let's keep it simple.) I will interweave the truck driver example throughout. Let's dive in!

Specific

You have to be as specific as possible! You want a raise? How much do you want? You want a promotion? Which job do you want? You want to be rich? How much is rich to you? Be specific! The more specific you can be, the greater the chance you will reach your goal! Being specific allows you to achieve your goal much quicker than you would have before! How does that happen? When you are specific, you can create a roadmap to see the progress you are making, and that will drive you to make better decisions, which will push you farther ahead in the end.

This will also allow you to celebrate your victories as you achieve them. The hardest part about achieving goals is the distance between checkpoints. The checkpoints that I am referring to are the mini victories along the way. These victories that help push us ahead to the next checkpoint. The more specific we can be, the more checkpoints we can have along the way, the more success we can feel, then the more we are going to want to continue striving and reaching for our goals. We have to be specific in order to feel the mini successes along the way to achieving our big goal. Without the checkpoints, we will be much more likely to perceive ourselves as failures when we don't succeed quickly enough. These common mistakes will impede progress and keep us from achieving our goal. The more specific you can be, the more likely you will achieve victory in life and business.

Using the truck driver example, how can he make his goal specific? We know he has to drive from point A to point B. Some people would set a goal of getting from A to B in 5 hours. At least that's a start. To make a specific goal, you might want to break up the trip into mini goals. Instead of the truck driver stating his goal from A to B, what if his goal was to go from A to D? So we are clear, B and D are the same place. Why do that? By making his goal look this way, he gave additional checkpoints along the way! Now he can be very specific as to the time goals from A to B, from

B to C, and then from C to D! Instead of thinking in terms of 5 hours, he will be thinking in terms of 1 – 2 hours. By breaking it up, he gave himself a more specific goal, and more leverage to hit his goal faster! How can you chunk down your goal to be more specific?

Measurable

Your goal has to be able to be measured. Achieving something that is not quantifiable is nearly impossible. Put a number to it or an amount. Avoid things like "I want to be rich." What does that mean? According to whose definition are we defining rich? How much is rich? Put a number to it. "I want $1 million." Now we are getting somewhere! When you put a quantity to it, then you have something concrete to strive for, not an abstract concept. Goals need to have some sort of measurement in order to monitor success and use it for guideposts along the way.

With our truck driver, he would need to make sure his goal was measurable. A weak goal might be to deliver his merchandise "today." A truly measurable goal would be to deliver his merchandise in 6 hours and be home by 5pm! Either way, you will get the job done (or not still have a job.) But in the second example, you will likely get it done faster and have more time for yourself after work!

Achievable

Achievable is a hard one. At some level, you want your goal to be outside your current level in order to stretch yourself to grow into the person who can achieve your goal. However, at its very core, a goal needs to be possible. I am not going to set a goal of walking on the moon, but can I do it? Yes, but it would completely take me off my current path, set me back another 10 years for training, and I would lose my livelihood along the way! That and I get sick flying in a plane, so I would not fare well in a spaceship! For me, walking on the moon would not be a realistically achievable goal!

What is your goal? Is it achievable? The only person who can decide whether your goal is achievable or not, is you. No one can set your goal for you. People try to, however! Without doubt, someone will try to put a limit on your goal. Maybe it's a well-intentioned family member or friend? Either way, the limit they impose on you has nothing to do with you, and everything to do with the limit they set for themselves! You have to ignore them! Rewrite your definition of achievable. If you have the will and the drive, it can be achieved!

If our truck driver set a goal to drive 5,000 miles in one day, would that be achievable? Definitely not (unless he was driving a rocket)! He needs to make sure that his goal has a possibility of being achieved. Could he drive 500 miles in a day? Absolutely!

How achievable is your goal? Do not let someone else define achievable for you! However, you still have to make sure you have a chance of succeeding. If you set a goal that is impossible (drive 5,000 miles in a day) to achieve, you will be setting yourself up for disappointment and resentment.

Relevant

How does your goal fit your current circumstances? With our truck driver, if he is supposed to drive 300 – 400 miles a day, would it make sense for him to have a goal of watching 8 hours of television tomorrow? No, because then he would miss work and potentially get fired! Relevant goals fit your current situation. In the scenario I just used, a good goal might be to drive his route without stopping in order to save time, get unloaded as fast and as safely as possible, and get home early. Notice the difference? Both were goals. One worked WITH the situation, one made the situation worse! How relevant is your goal? How can you make sure your goal will work within your situation to ensure best results?

Time-bound

With any goal, if you do not have a due date, you will find yourself off course, and doing things that do not further your goal! Set a due date! Researchers at Harvard Business School found that when they divided some students into three groups and let each group choose its deadline for their final papers, something profound happened (yet totally expected.) The group that set a deadline as the last day of term ended up doing the worst on their paper, because they left the assignment until the end of the term. The second group decided they needed to be done by midterm, and as expected, they did slightly better than the first group. The third group decided to have segmented due dates. They wanted to have the project broken up into parts, and specific parts had to be finished in regular intervals throughout the term. Not surprising, when they gave themselves specific dates and expectations of criteria being met, not only did they get their work done, it was also done better than the first two groups. They also found that the third group was able to get their final paper done quicker than the first two groups, and they reported that the project was easier to accomplish! Setting a date is powerful! It drives you to accomplish your goals, it helps you to achieve your goals faster, and it gives you a way to monitor your success along the way!

In this chapter you learned how to set a goal with full expectation of success. You learned that great goals need to be SMART (specific, measurable, achievable, relevant, and time-bound.) SMART goals ensure continued success in life and work! When you check objectives off your list, move on to the next goal. This keeps you always moving forward. Once you have achieved your goal, choose your next one! Make sure you celebrate your victories along the way. We should always either be in the middle of a goal or starting a new one. Make sure that you enjoy the process along the way!

CHAPTER 8

PAINT YOUR FUTURE PICTURE

"All I know,' said Candide, 'is that we must cultivate our garden."
~ Voltaire, Candide

What if there was a way to create your day? You could be the master architect, creating your day to go exactly as you want it to. Wouldn't that be great? As it turns out, you can! The latest research in neuroplasticity shows how powerful the mind can be in creating future situations. Neuroplasticity is simply the ability of the brain to adapt, grow, and change with each new stimulus applied. This new growth of neurons and change in the brain's circuitry has been seen with stroke patients who were told they would never be able to walk again (or do many normal functions, for that matter.) The process of neuroplasticity allows for the brain to re-wire itself to accommodate for the injured area. Over time, the brain will adapt, and then change, in order to bring functions back that were, 20 years ago, thought to be lost forever!

Fascinating stuff! If you want to read more about neuroplasticity you can go to "google scholar" (limits search to research articles) and see over 4,800 articles referencing neuroplasticity...since 2014!

Dr. Joe Dispenza has written about neuroplasticity and effect of mapping out your day in his book *Breaking the Habit of Being Yourself*. The major premise of his book is how we can, if we choose to, change or alter our reality by visualizing a better one! He walks through some fascinating research with amazing ramifications for our futures. No, I am not talking about some off-the-wall pseudoscience; I am talking about affirmations and visualizations. We are going to explore how these two simple concepts are used every day in the most successful people the world to bring their innermost dreams into their current reality. The best part is if they can do it, so can you!

If this is totally new to you, open your mind. Most people find this topic crazy when they first hear about it. I can assure you; the research is both extensive and effective. This method guarantees you will have a better day, week, year, and life—one that is less likely to be upset by randomness that affects many people in this world. Affirmations and visualizations are a dynamic method for paving your day and creating your circumstances.

This art is practiced by millions across the globe!

Affirmations

I ask you to think about the last time you felt confident in yourself. *Really confident.* So supremely confident, in fact, that you could take on any assignment your employer threw at you. So full of confidence that no matter the challenge, you would overcome any obstacle. Can you see it in your mind? Good. (If not, we will work on that in a minute.)

Now, what happened immediately before the confidence showed up? What were you doing? What were you thinking? What were you listening to? What stands out to you? Whether you are conscious to it or not, you probably had to "psych yourself up." In order to get supreme confidence, you need to pump yourself up. How do you do it? The act of "getting psyched up" is the process of using encouraging words, repeated over and over to give you the feeling of confidence. You might use words like "You are amazing! You are the best at what you do! You are the most qualified for this position!" These words you repeat to yourself are known as affirmations.

Affirmations are positive statements you say out loud

about yourself in an effort to encourage, motivate, inspire, and bring confidence in yourself to complete day-to-day tasks or responsibilities. How much better would your day be if in every conversation you had today, someone told you how you are amazing? We feel better when others tell us good things about ourselves. How much does your day currently seem like that? Unfortunately, your coworkers or friends might be having such a bad day, that they are all too willing to drag you down with them. You know what I'm talking about? The "Debbie Downers" of the world! They, for some reason, get joy out of life by stealing the joy from other people. Every time you leave a conversation with these people, you feel a little deader inside!

What is the difference between these two realities? Why is it that your well-being is generated based upon whether someone says something good or bad to you? The reason is so simple. THERE IS POWER IN THE SPOKEN WORD! Proverbs 18:21 says, "That tongue has the power of life and death, and those who love it will eat its fruit." Do you see it? The Bible shows us this principle! You can speak life into people by being encouraging and uplifting, or you can speak death by being negative and dejected! The choice is yours! So, how do affirmations play into this?

It does not matter if this spoken word comes from

someone else, or if it comes from you. The good news here is that you can be the one to say good things about yourself. It does not change the outcome. Just like the image of psyching yourself up, you can control your state of mind through affirmations. How do you do it? Take out five note cards. On these note cards, I want you to write five positive statements about yourself. Typically, you want to write these statements about the areas of your life where you need more confidence. Then, put these note cards somewhere you have to look at them every day (on a bathroom mirror, in your car, at workplace, etc.). Some examples of affirmations might be:

"I AM SUPREMELY CONFIDENT IN EVERYTHING I DO!"

"I HAVE EVERYTHING I NEED TO ACCOMPLISH MY GOALS/DREAMS!"

"I AM EXTREMELY LIKABLE AND PEOPLE LOVE MY COMPANY!"

"I AM AN AWESOME TEACHER AND MY STUDENTS LOVE LEARNING FROM ME!"

"I AM A BEAUTIFUL WOMAN WITH WELL-BEHAVED CHILDREN WHO ARE ATTENTIVE, HELPFUL, AND RESPECTFUL!"

The last thing to do is say each of these statements out loud to yourself (with meaning) five times a day, every day, for 30 days. At the end of 30 days, you will be amazed at how much more confidence you will have, and how much better your life has become. Do not wait for someone else to give you a compliment...Do it for yourself!

Visualizations

Visualizations go hand-in-hand with affirmations. Once you are able to speak powerful words or phrases to yourself, then you are ready for the next step. This will be painfully difficult for some of you. It was for me at the beginning. And at some level, it still is sometimes.

Visualization, very simply, is watching a mental movie of your day going EXACTLY how you want it to go. The best way I can describe visualization is through a personal experience. My first big health workshop was in the first office I worked in was scheduled to have over 60 people in attendance. I was nervous, to say the least. I had just started working on visualizations, so I decided to put it to the test. I spent an hour with my eyes closed, walking through my PowerPoint slides in my head, picturing how I was delivering the information to the people in the audience. However, I did not just want people hearing good advice. I wanted them to enjoy the message, be pumped up, and take action based off of what I was telling them. So, while I was visualizing myself delivering an amazing message, I pictured all the people in the audience smiling, having their full attention on me, taking notes, being energized and wanting to change their lifestyle. In this way, I was imagining a perfect scenario where everyone in attendance of the health workshop was enjoying the experience. Visualization works that way and is a powerful tool to be used. What you are doing is bringing into existence a desired outcome for an event. By seeing this desired outcome play out in your mind, you are creating a future where this will likely happen.

The day of the event, I delivered an amazing message; people were receptive and had a great time! Visualization helped me craft that outcome. This same thing can happen for you. No matter what event or circumstance you have coming up, you can apply this principle to help achieve a better outcome.

The process is actually quite simple. For example, take your day. You wake up tomorrow and the first thing you do, while your eyes are still closed, is walk through your day, making every situation a positive one. This sounds easier than it really is to do.

Walking through your day, you need to put a positive touch on every event that will be happening. What do I mean by walking through your day? Very simply, when walking through your day, imagine all the scenarios that you would want to have a positive outcome. Maybe the first interaction you have with a coworker? Maybe the meetings you have coming up today that you are nervous about? Maybe you have to give a presentation at work, and you are not sure about the possible outcomes? Use these examples to practice visualizations (or whatever you came up with) in order to craft your desired outcomes. Can you see how that can change the outcome of your day? How that could change the outcome of your week? How that could potentially change the outcome of the rest of your life? What is it going to hurt to try this? The worst-case scenario is that you feel more confident with your day. The best case scenario is that it will actually work, and you will actually craft the outcome of each interaction when you practice visualization! What do you have to lose? By practicing affirmations and visualizations, you will change the way you view your day, it will be easier for you to have more positivity in your life, and other people will notice and be magnetized by your positivity!

PART 3

DELIVERING THE GOODS

CHAPTER 9

DISCOVERING YOUR PASSION

"There is no passion to be found playing small—in settling for a life that is less than the one you are capable of living."
~ Nelson Mandela

Have you ever wondered how some people are excited to go to work each day, while others seem to have to be dragged out of bed kicking and screaming? What's the difference? How can two people go to the same work, do the same job, have the same boss, and have two completely different experiences? One is excited to go to work and the other is dreading it? When you can answer these questions, you will uncover the secret to happiness and a new level of engagement within your calling!

The objective in this chapter is two-fold. First, we need to walk through self-examination and the process of finding out what you enjoy doing in life. This helps because when you live out your passion and actually enjoy what you do, it no longer is considered work, but play. Also, when you enjoy what you are doing, it becomes a passion, and not a "job"!

Secondly, we need to assess your skills and/or natural abilities. God gifted you with a certain set of skills and abilities to match your passion. Therefore, if you figure out what you are good at, you are one step closer to finding your passion in life, and then you will be unstoppable!

The third thing to decipher is what personality type you have. Your personality will dictate what skills and direction would be best for your life. You do not have to follow this verbatim, but use it as an indicator of your best possible future. One example would be if you have a personality that craves attention and interaction with others, you would not want a desk job in a cubical that does not provide many opportunities to build relationships with others. By understanding your personality, you keep yourself from working or doing something that contradicts your strengths! Having a work setting you enjoy will ensure that you are HAPPY with your job!

The fourth thing we will uncover is what fires you up.

What gets you upset? What makes you uneasy? What part of the status quo do you not agree with? Your righteous anger with the status quo (or the way it is always done) indicates what you are passionate about. Again, when you find your passion, you will be one step away from massive success!

Lastly, we need to take all of this information and all of the principles that you will learn from this chapter and put it together to find out what your "God-Ordained Mission" in life should be! This final ingredient may be the most important one in "Discovering Your Passion"! All that being said, let's get started!

What do you enjoy doing most in life? No, I mean what is your favorite thing to do? What thing, if you got paid to do it, would cause you to quit your job and do that for the rest of your life? You know what I am talking about! What is it? Is it your past time activity? Is it reading? Is it writing books? Is it talking with friends? What is it for you? What would you do if you did not care what anyone else thought about you? Why aren't you doing it? What would you do even if you had to pay a huge sum of money to do it? Even if you had to save up for a year you would still do it. Even if you had to spend your yearly income on it, you would still do it! Do you have it in your mind, yet?

Knowing this information changes the game. Without this knowledge of yourself, you might be like the multitude of people who go their whole life without actually fulfilling their passion or purpose in life! DO NOT BE THAT PERSON! You will not be truly happy until you find your passion. When you find your passion, the next step is applying it! So how do you apply it?

Applying your passion takes self-analysis. What skills do you have that come naturally to you? Were you gifted in any way with a specific ability? What are you innately good at doing? What could you do without any thought, where other people struggle learning it? This could be your natural gifting, and therefore something that you could possibly be directed to do for a living. If this is your natural gift, it will also be fun for you to do!

Once you determine what your gifting is, then you can use that gifting for the betterment of others! The majority of small businesses got started by this principle. The person or people who started the company had a natural gifting (or incredible work ethic!) that she utilized to help others. In this way, you can monetize your gift to create a booming business that fills a need in others. The best businesses find what is needed most for other people and then fill that need with a product or service they created! They use the gift they were naturally imbued with. What is your gift? How can you use that gift to benefit others, and in the process, create a system that can profit you more than you could ever imagine?

A small sidebar needs to be said here. I am in no way saying that the reason you find your passion is to make money. What I am actually saying is that when you find your passion, money will naturally follow, because money is given based on value and worth, and when you follow your passion, you will create massive value for yourself and whatever service you provide! This is important, because if you do anything for money, your motivation is on material, and not helping others. Can you be successful when your main motivation is money? Of course, but that will always be short term success. The only way to have lasting success and happiness is to be motivated by filling the needs of others in a substantial and meaningful way. This will ensure two things: you stay motivated, even when things get tough, and that you will experience huge wealth! The wealth that I am speaking of refers to both money, and more importantly, the fulfillment reflected when you satisfy others' needs! Keep that in mind when you are finding your passion...what are you doing it for? Make sure your motivation is in line with your core values and then success and happiness is bound to follow!

The next thing to look at is your personality type. When "Discovering Your Passion," your personality type needs to be taken into consideration because if you find something you are good at, even naturally talented and gifted in, but it goes against your personality traits, then you will be swimming upstream in your attempt to become successful. How? Say you are an outgoing person who loves to have fun, interact with people, and thrive on relationships in the workplace. Then, let's say that you are naturally talented with numbers. You get math better than anyone you know. You are a genius with calculations and extrapolations of figures and charts and graphs. Then, because of your work in this chapter, you decide that because of this gifting, you should go back to school to be an accountant, because accountants work with numbers and charts all day long. More than likely this will make you miserable. Why? Accountants usually work alone, spend long hours in front of a computer, and may go weeks without actually talking to their clients! You did not realize this when you started college, so when you graduate and enter the work force, you hate what you do because of the complete isolation that comes with the gig! How could that have been prevented? Know your personality! You would not want to be an accountant in that example. Your personality would more likely fit someone in the spotlight, working hand in hand with other people. So how would knowing your personality help you continue working within your gifting, but not fall into the trap of a job you are doomed to not enjoy from the start?

By doing a personality test to determine what your strengths and weaknesses are, you can create a job that falls within those strengths and avoids the weaknesses so you can ultimately be happy....which will result in better work and greater fulfillment. In the previous example, the perfect position would not be a number cruncher in a secluded office, but maybe someone who teaches financial management to large groups of people, like with Financial Peace University™. You would be more fulfilled and happy teaching and working with real people in a continuously fluid work experience. This will keep you motivated and successful, because you are within your strengths and avoiding your weaknesses!

What you want to do is find an online test to determine your personality. The test that I use with my team members is the DISC profile. You can find free DISC tests online that will give you the results and some resources to help with your strengths and weaknesses. The DISC profile will be the best first test to point you in the right starting point to move away from a boring, unfulfilling job, and into something that moves the needle and keeps you happy. As a result, you will become the successful person that you want to be!

What fires you up? What irritates you about your current situation? What injustice in our society really gets you going? What things can raise your blood pressure in two seconds, and gets you on a tirade/soap box? In what ways do you preach to others about this injustice? Is there something wrong with our world that creates unease within your soul? Your answers to these questions create something inside you called a "holy discontent."

A holy discontent is something that cannot be rationalized away. No amount of talking or reasoning will ever have you feel alright with the situation. An example of this is Mother Teresa. Mother Teresa had a passion for helping soothe other people's suffering. She spent most of her life helping people who had no means of helping themselves. She went to the most destitute region of Calcutta, India, to help people in the slums. She formed a group of people who devoted their lives to changing others', and in the process, changed the world! She had a holy discontent! She stopped at nothing to be the solution for the problem that troubled her soul.

What is that for you? In what way are you troubled by

some current situation or circumstance? Are you possibly the solution? Could you solve the problem with your natural talent and gifting? If so, you could be the change that the world needs! You could be the light for others desperately in need. In the process, people are going to want to join you in your cause. LET THEM! You need the help anyway, so let others join your cause. If you are really on to something, people will want to help. A good metric to use to see if you are on the right track is the willingness of people to help you. Many people are looking for a good cause to join, and your cause could be a great one. If so, people are going to want to join in and help. What you need to do is create a way to let other people inside! Then, with a group of people helping, you can change the world!

We just walked through the process of "Discovering Your Passion." The last step is to add up all this information to see your ultimate position. Maybe it is a job or occupation somewhere that would be perfect for what you enjoy doing, fits within your gifting and natural abilities, fits your personality type, and fulfills the holy discontent in your soul! When you find that position, you will spend the rest of your life on fire with passion, and achieve your God-ordained purpose on this planet. Maybe there isn't such a job created yet. Guess what? You can create it! Who says you can't just create the business so that you can have the job of your dreams? Be the change you want to see in the world! Create the business. Create your perfect position! God has put you here with all of your quirks and passions and holy discontent so that you can have an impact on society. DO NOT PLAY SMALL! Make the decision to change this world. Only you can do it. Only you have the ability. Only you have the gifting. Only you have the passion that can do it. Only you can motivate other people to join your cause. Try to create the business and be happy with the rest of your life. The choice is yours! Either way, if you stay the same and do not make the necessary changes in your own life, you will not have the amazing life you want and are striving for. Please, make the change, for our world's sake!

CHAPTER 10

DON'T TOE THE WATER

*"You can never cross the ocean until you have
the courage to lose sight of the shore."*
~ Christopher Columbus

Have you ever heard the phrase, "Don't toe the water"? Did you stop and think about what it means? If you think about it for a minute, and how it applies to your life, you will see the parallel and why it is so vastly important to living your dreams and achieving massive success. The best way to explain this concept is with an example from my childhood. When I was growing up, we had a pool in our back yard. In the spring, my father would start the process of turning the heaters on and de-icing the water (I grew up in North Dakota, so winter was 7 months long and had temps below zero for months at a time!). Come April, he would say that we could swim, but it would be "chilly." Keep in mind, we would still sometimes get snow in April, so the temperature was not that high. When my friends came over to swim (when you were the kid with the pool, everyone wanted a piece of you), one of two things would happen. One, we would all run and jump into the pool, freeze our butts off for a couple minutes, get used to it, and have a blast playing for the next couple of hours. Or two, we would stick our toe into the water, feel how cold it was, and decide to not swim, completely missing out on the amazing fun that we would have experienced had we just jumped in. The point? What experiences are you missing out on because you are busy toeing the water? In what areas of your life are you letting others have the fun and amazing experience because you are playing cautious? What is the worst that could happen if you just jumped in head first? When I jumped in, there was no turning back! What if you jumped in? There would be no going back to the life of toeing the water! No going back to the mundane existence that you once knew. What is the worst thing that could happen by jumping in head first? What is the best thing that could change your life forever? In my experience, jumping in head first is more likely to result in your best experiences, instead of negative ones. Are you ready to stop toeing the water and jump in? Go for it, jump in!

The "toeing the water" analogy expresses and describes

the importance of giving everything you have to your purpose. What I want for you is to experience the joy that comes from giving your all to a project or purpose, in order to feel the full expression of happiness that comes with it. Either you are willing to go "all in" or you need to get out! If you are not willing to give your all to what you do, then you are in the wrong field. You shouldn't need to have your arm twisted in order to give your all! If you still need help with this concept, go back and reread the last chapter to discover your passion in life, so that once attained, you can learn the principle of "all in"!

How can you become all-consumed with your passion (without neglecting your family or God, of course?) I will walk you through the principles of becoming a full-out, all-consumed, "crazy for your cause" individual that wins in life because you are fighting for a cause bigger than yourself! Also, I will show you how to ensure that you are moving toward your goals based on the decisions you make every day, instead of away from your goals like many people do that aren't using these strategies.

Lastly, we will discuss the concept of no distractions. We will look at your life and identify the places that are pulling you away from your goals and trying to keep you from achieving the success you are working towards. By eliminating your distractions, there will be nothing standing in your way. You will have the extra time, the extra energy, and the extra will power to achieve all that you set out to achieve!

Are You In The Furnace?

Do you know if you are you "all-in"? Do you have an unrelenting passion for what you do? Do people around you comment on how dedicated you are to what you do? Does your boss notice? Does your family notice? Does God notice? If you answered yes to these questions, that means you are "all in"! If you answered no, don't worry. Remember, you can always change. You can, in a moment, decide to give your all to what you are doing. If you cannot give your all, perhaps you need to re-assess if that is where you are supposed to be! Go back to chapter 9 to figure out where your talents would be better utilized. After evaluating your situation and finding your best usage of your skills, immediately move in that direction! This action is pivotal to creating your success.

An example of being "all-in" is in the "Book of Daniel" in the *Old Testament*. In Daniel 3, the king, Nebuchadnezzar, ordered a gold statue of him be made, and pursuant to the law, any time the bell rung, everyone would have to stop what they were doing, bow down and worship his statue. Anyone caught not worshipping his idol, or who worshiped any other god, were thrown into a burning furnace.

At that time, King Nebuchadnezzar had appointed three Jewish men to leadership roles in Babylon. The three men, Shadrach, Meshach and Abednego, refused to worship the idol of the king, and openly continued worshiping God. Some of the kings' men saw them and reported the three to King Nebuchadnezzar. He was "furious with rage" (Dan. 3:13) and had the three brought before him. He quite frankly told them that they had one more chance to bow down and worship him or he would have them thrown into the furnace to be burned alive. Shadrach, Meshach, and Abednego replied to him, "King Nebuchadnezzar, we do not need to defend ourselves before you in this matter. If we are thrown into the blazing furnace, the God we serve is able to deliver us from it, and he will deliver us from Your Majesty's hand. But even if he does not, we want you to know, Your Majesty that we will not serve your gods or worship the image of gold you have set up." (Dan. 3: 16-18)

Shadrach, Meshach and Abednego have taken their stance. They will not budge on this. They are unswerving in their faith. They are unwavering in their pursuit of their passion. They are unrelenting in their principles. Because of this, they are going to be thrown into a fiery furnace to be burned alive! How many of us would go that far? Would you be willing to be thrown into a furnace for your beliefs or principles? Would you stand firm when others are bending or breaking? If yes, then you are on the right path to success! Do you really have to worry about that today, being thrown into a burning furnace? Of course not! However, the point is the same. Are you giving 100% of yourself into what you are doing, or are you toeing the water? These three men are giving all of themselves to their mission, and watch the results!

The king was furious with their proclamation that they will not now, nor ever, worship him or his idols. As a result, they are sentenced to be thrown into the fire. The king is so upset that he tells his people to turn up the furnace to seven times hotter than usual. The furnace was so hot that the people responsible for throwing Shadrach, Meshach and Abednego into the fire were burned alive for standing too close! That's hot!

The amazing part of the story is God actually saved them from the fire! He sent an angel down to rescue them from the flames. The king said "weren't there three men that we tied up and threw into the fire?" His men told him there were indeed three men thrown into the fire. What he said next is mind blowing! "Look! I see four men walking around in the fire, unbound and unharmed, and the fourth looks like a son of the gods." (Dan. 3: 24, 25) King Nebuchadnezzar could actually see the angel in the fire with Shadrach, Meshach and Abednego! The king then calls them out of the fire, and they walked out unharmed. "They saw that the fire had not harmed their bodies, nor was a hair of their heads singed; their robes were not scorched, and there was no smell of fire on them." (Dan. 3: 27)

The point of the story isn't to tell you how amazing our God is, because we probably know that and remember that from Sunday school. The point here illustrates for you what IS possible when you go all in! Shadrach, Meshach, and Abednego were willing to be thrown into a burning furnace for their principles and mission and were unwilling to back down. As a result of that passion, when the king took them out of the fire, he issued a decree that any person who defiled the God of Shadrach, Meshach, and Abednego would be killed and their house burned down! What an amazing turn of events, and it all happened because the three men were willing to die for their purpose, instead of giving in to the temptation of fitting in and going with status quo. People who follow the status quo NEVER change the world!

All-Consuming Mission!

Are you all-consumed with your mission? Is every breath out of your mouth about your passion and purpose? Are you constantly and consistently trying to bring people over to your truth? Are you relentless in the pursuit of your passion, so much so that people notice and commend you on it? If not, then that is the next thing to overcome, because unless you are all-consumed with your passion, you will not be able to make the necessary sacrifices and take the steps to become massively successful!

Before you can become all-consumed you need grasp a couple of key concepts. The first thing to understand is that people who are all-consumed want to talk about nothing other than their passion. They do not waste a perfect opportunity to talk about their mission on a topic like the weather or sports! These people, if you try to pull them off-topic, will do everything in their power to get back to the most important thing to them, which is their mission. Because of this, they are always marketing themselves to the people around them. All-consumed people struggle making small-talk. Not that they can't do it, and not that you shouldn't ever talk about the weather, you just lose interest in the things that do not really matter. This first sign that you are all-consumed is massively important. Don't be dismayed if you aren't there yet. You can start getting there by controlling your conversations and directing them to your mission and passion.

The second point to understand about people that are all consumed is that they do not take "holidays." They do not take weekends off; they do not take their 15 minute breaks every hour. Also, they work late without expectation of more pay! Hopefully if you are still reading this book, you have gathered that in order to be successful, you cannot be like the 95% of people who expect to get all of the above. Wait, they do not expect it, they think they DESERVE it! People who are all-consumed know that the only thing they deserve is what they are willing to work to achieve. As a result, success and happiness follow. The reason why so many people are struggling with their lives is because they walk around every day without passion, expecting to get more than they have worked for, and are upset that they haven't been given more (we know these people are miserable because anti-depressant drugs are a multi-billion dollar a year industry.) What part of that makes sense? NONE OF IT DOES! Please, do not be that person! At all cost you need to break yourself of that habit. Start working in this new direction. The more you become all-consumed with your mission, the more success will follow, and the more you will want to be consumed! This feedback loop will ensure future positive success!

One thing to keep in mind is that people who are all-consumed are still able to have fun. Being all-consumed does not mean that you will never be able to have a good time again. What you will find, however, is that you can have fun, just not at the expense of your mission! Experiencing this is a wonderful feeling, because when you get to this point you know that you are all-consumed!

Let's revisit an action step from chapter 6 on "Disciplining Yourself." Do you remember your notecard? Hopefully you have already started writing your top three to five priorities on a notecard to help guide you and ensure your essential tasks are done in a timely manner. What I want to do is paint a picture as to why you would want to make a notecard with your top priorities. As you know, there are only a finite number of hours in a day. That being said, why is it that some people get more done with the same amount of time than others? Have you ever stopped to figure out how that could be possible? These people do not sacrifice the few great things for the many good things. We all have a list of 50 things to do in a day, but how we choose what to do is where the success happens. It all comes down to choice! You get to choose whether you invest your time on what will propel you toward your goals and are aligned with your mission, or you will choose to spend your time doing things that will pull you away from your mission (even if it is a good idea.)

Did you notice the difference? One option is an investment into your future, because it will bring an increased return for you, while the other is an expense, meaning once it is gone, you will not get it back! You need to always evaluate your choices. Which ways can you change the decisions you make so that they better line up with your mission or passion? What choices do you make every day that pull you from your mission? When you can identify the great choices that propel you toward your goals, and stay away from the good choices (or bad choices) that pull you away from your mission, you will be shot like a missile toward victory over your situation and in life.

No Distractions!

The last part of the process you must go through in order to have the life of your dreams, achieve massive success, and hit all your goals which will fulfill your mission is eliminating your distractions! Sounds easy, doesn't it? For a lot of people this is the hardest challenge in the book. It might be for you as well. Many people find peace when eliminating the things that distract them. Usually people find they have more time, and therefore, more energy that can be utilized in fulfilling their goals when they eliminate the distractions. Distractions always pull effort away from your goals! Eliminating your distractions is vital to achieving success on huge level.

Where are your distractions? What things have a hold on you and keep you from getting things done? What things occupy your mind when you are supposed to be getting work done? Do you have toys (cell phone, television, video games, social media, etc.) that are pulling your attention away from your responsibilities? If you found out all the time you were wasting on these things, you would more than likely eliminate some of them from your life over-night. However, many people don't realize how much time they waste on them, and therefore, will not get rid of them without being shown how detrimental they are to success. When some people read this, they will think "I don't have any of those things" or "I don't have THAT big of a problem, I just spend a couple of minutes a day on social media, phone, or computer." The first step in identifying the problem is admitting you have a problem! For the next couple of days, every time you get on a social media website, log how much time you spend. You may only get on a social media website for five minutes at a time, which is not that much in the grand scheme of life, but how many times a day do you get on total? Three times a day? Five times a day? Ten times a day? When you add up twelve times of five minutes apiece, that's an hour of time a day that you wasted on something that does not propel you toward your goals and dreams! Can you see the importance of identifying your distractions? BE HONEST WITH YOURSELF!! The only one looking at this is you. Please stop rationalizing your wasted time. Social media is not a necessity. Sitting on the internet on your phone is not a necessity. Television is not a necessity. Successful people DO NOT watch ten hours of television per week. How much time do you watch TV? Write down how much time you spend on these categories (and others if you have another vice) and create a time log of all the time you might be wasting on fruitless activities. You will quickly see how you can create the time necessary to get your responsibilities done.

Please hear me; I am not telling you to throw away your television, or computer, or phone. Well, for some of you, you might need to throw the TV away! For most of you, spending a few hours per week on television is alright. For some people, however, the do not have one show they watch per week (which is usually one hour), but one show each night! You have a different show for each night of the week. Let's see an example of this from my life.

When my wife and I were first married, we decided that we didn't want to get cable TV, because we did not want to waste our time together watching the television. We went a long time without watching TV, and it was great! We had tons of time! Then, in our infinite wisdom, we decided to get limited basic television. It only had three or four channels, so we could watch one particular show. I believe it was *One Tree Hill* on the CW (if you were curious.) We started with the intention of only watching one show per week, which was one hour long. What happened stunned us and caught us off guard! Before long, we each had a show every night, which turned into one hour of TV per night per person! What started as a one hour a week commitment, which we were going to do together as a couple, ended up with multiple one hour commitments per week, and much of it was spent without the other person! In the end, we decided that we needed to get rid of the cable, because it was wasting too much time, and more importantly, we were being pulled apart. We were more interested in the show on TV than with spending time with each other. How many people does that happen to? Too many, by my count! Maybe that is happening to you right now. You can get rid of the distraction to not just your mission, but your life as well! Act now. Get rid of the cable. (At the very least create a schedule of when it is appropriate for you to watch the television without pulling too much time from your responsibilities.) You can always rent movies for a date night (or fun night, if you are single), but the TV will just distract you from where you want to be with your life/work/dreams/goals.

You now understand the principles of going all-in, becoming all-consumed, writing your top priorities on a note card, and eliminating all distractions. Now you are ready for the next step, which is to "Become a Master!"

CHAPTER 11

BECOMING A MASTER

"I've been waiting for you, Obi-Wan. We meet again, at last. The circle is now complete. When I left you, I was but the learner; now I am the master."

~ Darth Vader

Becoming a master is critical in the pursuit of success. According to Merriam-Webster, mastery is defined as possession or display of great skill or technique, and secondly as having the upper hand in a contest or competition. If you are planning on succeeding in life (which you wouldn't be reading this book if you weren't interested,) then possessing great skill and technique is a crucial ingredient on that path! I love the second half of the definition, "having the upper hand in a contest or competition." Why is that important? The master doesn't take second place! The master is a winner, who keeps developing his/her skills in order to be the best. Before that happens, we need to figure out a couple of things. First, how does a person develop a skill? Second, what do we do with that skill once it is developed? Third, do we need to do it all by ourselves, or can we ask for help?

Before we begin, I need to point out a couple simple observations you might infer about the forthcoming information. These principles have a lot of leeway. There will be plenty of opportunity to interpret and apply these principles to the yardstick that is your life. "Becoming a Master" doesn't have a "one size fits all" explanation. You will have to cull this down to fit your needs. I've written this chapter in a way so as to give you the ability to seek out your best resources to accomplish the task of mastery.

Put In Your Time

The first step on this journey to mastery is spending the necessary time to become a master. In the book *Outliers*, Malcolm Gladwell put it best with the concept of 10,000 hours being necessary to become a master! Many people in this world are not prepared, nor do they want to put in the 10,000 hours it takes to develop and become a master. The ownership has been put squarely back on each individual's shoulders and evens the playing field for all people. You can be as good as you want to be.

Natural ability never trumps hard work. 10,000 hours is the great equalizer! You could have absolutely no talent in a certain field, but if you are willing to put in 10,000 hours, you will still develop a mastery over your industry or field.

I can tell you with utmost certainty that anyone who has put in their 10,000 hours to become a master despises hearing someone discount their hard work, blood, sweat, and tears as "talent and natural ability"! Larry Bird exemplifies this quality. Larry Bird played for the Boston Celtics and is one of basketball's greatest players of all time. He will always be remembered for his three point shooting, incredibly high free throw shooting percentage (still is among all-time greatest, even 20+ years after he retired), and a tenacity for winning over all adversity! How did he achieve that status? Was he born with it? Was it just natural talent and ability? You decide for yourself after I walk you through his 10,000 hours (and many more).

Larry Bird was a 12-time NBA All-star, 3-time NBA MVP, Hall of Fame inductee, and won multiple championships. However, before all that happened, he was putting in his 10,000 hours to become a master. One of my favorite stories about Larry Bird was told by a coach of another team. This coach brought one of his rookie players to the gym hours before their game against the Boston Celtics to teach this rookie how mastery is developed. The whole trip there, the coach is explaining to this rookie how Larry Bird puts in extra time each day to not just be a great player but to be the best player each game! The coach and his player walk onto the court six hours early for the game, and the court is empty! No one is there! This rookie, thinking his coach was crazy and that no one really comes to the gym six hours early, starts talking trash to his coach, saying "See coach, no one is that crazy to come six hours early before a game. He's probably at home, sitting on his couch, watching television." The coach knew he wouldn't find Larry Bird on the court. The coach looked at his rookie, smiled, and pointed to the nose-bleed section of the Celtics arena. Way up at the top section of the gym, Larry was running laps to get his cardio workout before coming down to the court to work on his shooting! Larry Bird would run for 30 minutes to an hour before he ever came down to the court. The rookie learned that in order to be the best, you have to go above and beyond what everyone else is doing. The reason Larry Bird was better than everyone else was because he worked harder, put in more quality time, and decided in his spirit that he would do whatever it took to be the best, which increased his chances of winning in the game of life!

Larry Bird was definitely not the most athletic player on

the court. He overcame his deficits of athleticism by working harder and smarter than anyone else. Larry was known as a mental ninja. He understood that the game of basketball was not just an athletic competition, but also a mental game. Larry Bird was the type of person who fundamentally understood that his mind controls his body. He was amazing at breaking down limiting beliefs that would cripple other people. He had a mastery over his physical limitations, so instead of letting those limitations stunt his capacity for growth, he used his mind to increase his potential by finding ways to maximize his strengths in order to minimize his weaknesses. He was not the quickest player on the court, so in order to overcome this weakness, he would study his opponent (whichever person he would be guarding during the game), learn all of that player's strengths, which way does he like to drive to the basket (right-handed or left-handed), does he like to shoot jump shots or three pointers, etc. Once he learned absolutely everything he could about that person's basketball skill, then he seemed to know what the other player was going to do before the other player even knew what he was going to do! This allowed him to increase his quickness by being in the right place before he even was supposed to be there! How's that for mastery?

The most important part of becoming a master is training. The single greatest way to push past the crowd of people who are in your workplace and become the best is through consistent training. However, doing the extra work and going the extra mile is seen as difficult. As a result of that level of thinking, many people are unwilling to do the extra work it takes to become a master. If you truly want to have your goals and dreams accomplished in life, then expect to put in the extra work it takes to develop mastery! The best part, if you are in the field that you are passionate about, it will not seem like work. It will be the best part of your day, doing those things that propel you on to success and happiness! What did Larry Bird do to develop mastery?

Larry would show up hours early for game day. Keep in mind, he put in his 10,000+ hours of work in long before this point. Even after attaining his level of master, he still put in extra time. Everyone is a master at some level once they reach the NBA. So how does a master elevate above other masters? Larry was known for his amazing ability to drain three pointers in clutch moments of games to help his team win numerous games. That being said, when practicing, he wouldn't start by shooting threes. In fact, he would not even shoot a three pointer until he had made hundreds of shots from a couple of feet away from the hoop. He would start directly under the hoop, and his goal was to make three shots in a row with the ball going through the hoop without having the ball touch the rim! Think about that. What an amazing skill to develop. Doing that once is hard, let alone three times in a row! Larry would do that from three spots on the court (right side of the hoop, middle of the lane, and left side of the hoop.) Once he made three in a row from these three spots, he would back up a step and do it again. Once he would make three in a row again, he would back up a step. Larry would do this until he made it out to the three point line. When you do the math that equates to roughly 63 shots made without having the ball touch the rim! Believe me when I say he did not get through in just the minimum 63 shots! That means Larry has shot a couple hundred shots in a row, just to warm up and get his shooting touch ready. Most players try to just walk out on the court and start shooting. Most players will never become a champion either! Are you willing to do the extra work? Are you going to go the extra mile to become the master you could become? Are you willing to leave your coworkers behind, to walk out of the crowd, to start leading instead of following? Champions lead. Champions are always out in front, leading others! Part of mastery is leading others by being the person they can look up to and try to follow after!

"Becoming a Master" also means having a commitment to quality work. What good is it to work hard, put in 10,000 hours, and train harder than anyone when the quality of the work is not up to snuff? Why put in all that time if you do not have pride in your work? The most vital element that all masters have is pride in the quality of their work! They may not always get the most done, but what they do get done is always the best. Masters have an innate ability to not just get the job done, but get it done the right way, with efficiency and extremely high quality. Picture that person who sits in the master chair at your workplace. I would imagine that person is not always flashy about it, but that his/her work stands on its own. Masters have impeccable workmanship and quality that is unsurpassed by anyone else...and masters like it that way! They pride themselves on being the best and producing the best quality work because that is the level of expectation they place on themselves! The prize is not in getting work done, but getting it done to perfection. Not to say that masters are perfect. Far from it. What I mean is that masters strive for perfection in everything they do. How about you? Do you strive for perfection, or are you ok with average? These questions are deliberately tough and meant to get to the heart of the matter. No matter how you answer these questions presently, you can always change yourself for the better. Tomorrow can be and is a new day! Make the change! Be the person who becomes a master. It will be the best decision you have ever made!

Once you make the decision to improve the quality of your work, be ready. Other people will start to notice. You need to be excited about that, because it means you are on the right path...the path to leadership! What comes next is the leadership mantle. Accept it graciously. When the quality of your work improves and others start noticing you, they will likely come and ask you for help. When you develop mastery, others will want to follow you! They will want to be like you. When you accept this role, automatically you begin to experience change. The change I'm referring to is the growth of the leader inside of you. What a great feeling!

One thing to keep in mind throughout this whole experience of mastery is humility! Always remember, you were once in their place. You were not always the top dog. You, at one time, were asking the same questions they are asking you now! Stay humble, and help them the way this book has helped you! The best characteristic for an organization to grow is to have a group of committed people willing to help others develop, which helps the company grow.

Core Values

What are you core values? What are the codes that you live by? What, if any, rules dictate how you live and who you are as a person? The answers to these questions are so important because they shape who you will become on the journey to mastery! If you have not written down your core values, make the time right now to do it. What things are absolutes in your life? God? Family? Friends? Fun? Write out those three or four things that are most important to you and are ones you would not go against for any amount of money. What you write down are your core values. Your core values act as your North Star, your compass. I'll share my core values with you for some context:

1. Integrity
2. Congruency
3. Work Ethic
4. Excellence
5. Justice

Now that you've seen mine, what are yours? They can be one word answers, or sentences. Core values are extremely personal to you, meaning only you can decide. Once you have your core values, you will know how to best motivate yourself when the training and mastery gets tough. These core values are what push you toward victory and success in life and work, and these core values will always be with you. These are not to be taken lightly! Ask someone to help you; choose someone who knows you well. You will be able to come up with them easier with that person as your sounding board. Also, with someone on board with you in this journey, he/she will be more likely to push you to succeed, because both of you will feel part of the process! Let your person come along with you on your mission! I think you will love the results!

Last thing in the journey to mastery is getting a coach. You need people in your life who have been where you are and know how to get past the hurdles that you are about to face (or are currently facing.) All the best and brightest people have coaches who help them along the way. As I mentioned previously in chapter 5, Tiger Woods has a coach for all facets of his game. If the best golfer in the history of the game still has coaches, you probably should too!

Who should be your coach/mentor? My advice would be to find someone in your organization who would have gone through similar challenges to the ones that you will face. Your mentor will be your greatest asset on this journey of growth and development. A coach will help you in areas that you did not even realize were problems. Most importantly, a coach will point out your blind spots! What is a blind spot? Let's picture driving a car. On your car, the rear-view mirrors are there to show you who is behind you. However, the mirrors can only show you so much.

The mirrors only show you behind the car because the makers of the car assume you can always turn your head to see next to you. The problem occurs when you look at your mirrors and assume no one is beside you as well. That causes a collision because the car was hiding in your blind spot and you as the driver did not even notice it was there. It should be fairly self-explanatory why pointing out a blind-spot is important. Because, just like driving, if you turn without seeing these blind spots, you are likely to crash your car (or life/job) in the process, all because you did not see what was there! You need to see your coach as your all-ways mirror. Not only will a coach point out what you cannot see for yourself, but also what you do not WANT to see, due to all the things we discussed in the first five chapters of this book. (You might have overcome some of your most pressing issues but more will come, especially when you are trying to develop mastery!) Being prepared for setbacks is the job of your coach. He/she will help you see the fall that is coming and help soften the blow if it does come. Mastery doesn't prevent the occasional failure. You want to make sure that the fall is minimal, and you keep moving up and forward in life and with your subsequent successes!

You now have everything that you will need to become the master you were born to be! The question is will you take the action necessary to develop mastery? Anyone has the ability and the calling to become a master...if you want it! Unfortunately, we have only a few masters and a lot of quitters! Please do not be a quitter. I am begging you to stick with it. You are closer than you ever imagined. Be the person who becomes the master. We need your mastery more than you know!

CHAPTER 12

CREATING YOUR CULTURE

*"Our lives begin to end the day we become
silent about things that matter."*
~ Martin Luther King, Jr.

This chapter is the last and most important chapter in this book! Very few things in life are more valuable to an individual than his/her culture. We are going to walk through what it takes to create a culture that people are going to want to adapt as their own, and also one that your family and other loved ones will want to follow for generations to come! Where do we start?

"Creating Your Culture" starts by telling other people what you are passion about. It should never be hard to tell people about your passion. Also, you should never have to filter your passion for what other people think! Your passion (or mission) is what drives you to success. Why would you NOT want to talk about it with everyone? Let other people hear about your passion. Don't worry about whether someone will like your passion or not. Passionate people ignite the passion in others, which gives them the motivation to want more out of life! We need more people led by passion. We have too many people who are led by their head and not their heart! Imagine a world with more people being led by their passion? There would be less stress, more enjoyment, greater fulfillment, and an overall better quality of work that would penetrate all markets. Being led by passion, in my opinion, is severely lacking in our country today.

What does "Being the Voice" of your mission look like? What does that mean? When you are being the voice, you are a walking, talking billboard of your passion and mission that other people can see. Being the voice is a chosen act, a willful desire to inspire others around your core principles. People see your passion, and want what you have, because they will see intrinsic value in it. What is the value in other people seeing you as a passionate, mission-driven person? Other people will value you as someone who lives his/her life based on core principles that are unshakeable. Having unshakeable core principles is very inspiring for other people, because sticking to your principles isn't easy. The easy thing to do is change your principles to match the current thinking. In the midst of people changing their principles, how can you stay strong in what you believe?

A great example of a person who exemplified unwavering, unshakeable dedication to his purpose and core principles is Martin Luther King, Jr. Racial equality was his life's passion and calling from God, and he fulfilled that calling with every breath until his death!

Martin Luther King, Jr. had an ability to motivate people to his calling. He was an extremely influential person. While in college, he was noted many times as someone who liked the lime light, wanted to party, and was always the center of attention. At that point in his life, he did not have any passion for what he was doing. He was doing what his father before him, and his grandfather before that had done. He was going through the motions (and making sure to have fun while doing it). Does that sound familiar? In some ways, are you just going through the motions in your life? What has to change for you to step into your passionate calling from God? MLK, Jr. had that moment in college when he saw the racial injustice that was happening all around the country.

For the most part, up until then, MLK, Jr. had spent the majority of his life separated from what was happening in the world. He went to school at an almost entirely black college. He could not see (or feel) the injustice that others felt. Once he felt that injustice, however, the course of his life changed drastically! No longer could he ignore what was happening. No longer could he sit on the sidelines of life. No longer could he have fun while others suffered. The status quo was not acceptable for him, and he had a deep desire (mission) to change that status quo. This started his mission to change our country's culture to racial equality instead of racial injustice.

What a great example of having a holy discontent! MLK, Jr. couldn't live with the world the way it was so he decided it was his responsibility to change the current belief system that was held in place. Do you think it was easy? Of course not, but when you have a holy discontent your major concern is culture change, not whether it will be easy!

Would you die for your core principles? If your life was threatened, would you, instead of having an unwavering core, change in order to save your life? How many people would change their principles (eternal) in order to save their life (temporary)? How many people do not realize that what you believe lasts forever, while your life is fleeting? Have you ever thought about that? The beliefs you hold are what people remember about you. People will have a harder time remembering what you looked like, what cars you drove, the house you lived in, than they will remembering the core principles you lived by. Are you living your life with that in mind? What do you want people to remember about you? If you died today, how long would it take for people to forget you? Please, do not let this make you depressed! This example simply shows you how much more there is for your life. Remembering someone that stood for his/her core principles is easy. Why? Because too often people live their lives without any core principles, so the people who follow their core principles stand above the rest. Too few people live for a set of core principles. So, when you have that person who lives and breathes his core principles, standing out in the crowd of people that float by in life becomes easy! That was MLK, Jr. He stood firm on the fact that all people were created equal. He eventually died for that belief. What is the legacy that he left? He changed culture in the United States! That happened because of his unshakeable commitment to his core principles.

MLK, Jr., over the course of his life, spoke publicly over 2500 times. His "career" lasted about 10 years. If you do that math that means that he spoke around 250 times each year until his death. If you take into account that his speaking engagements were usually in different cities, he worked almost year round without time off. He did not have time to take a vacation! He had too much work to do. He was consumed with his mission. People needed to hear about racial equality! He was called to his mission. He had a job to do, and he felt that he was the only one who could do it. He was the foundation of the civil rights movement. People looked for him to be the rock, the anchor for others to cling to when the seas got rough. Were there times when he wanted to quit? Of course there were. Was there frustration along the way? Undoubtedly! Did that stop him? NO!

Are you an anchor for your passion? Are you the pillar of excellence that other people want to follow? Would you want to follow you? These questions are good to use as a tester to see where you are currently with your mission. If you do not like your answers to these questions, then change where you are at! The best part about changing your current position is just making the decision to change. Once you make the decision to change, it is done. Your mind will always bring to reality those decisions you have set internally. Make the decision to change, and see what happens!

According to a CNN report done in August of 2011 on *23 traits of good leaders,* leaders have consistent character traits that can be explored. Of the 23 character traits, 8 jumped off the page. You will see a mirror to some of the principles discussed in this book.

1. Passion
2. Confidence
3. Clarity (of your purpose)
4. Integrity
5. Compassion for others
6. Humility
7. Empower others to succeed
8. Collaborative (work well with others)

What an awesome list! These 8 character traits have been discussed at length in this book. As I have said many times, you can change in a second. With this list, you can work to become the leader that your family, company, community, and world needs. When you change, others will want to change with you. A culture changes when multiple people change. After you change, how will you help others to change with you?

Do you allow room for others to join your mission? How much more could you accomplish if you let other people join your mission? What is stopping you from letting other people join you? Do you have a fear of leadership? Or do you think that you can do it all on your own? Whatever it is, in order for you to take the next step towards completing your calling is to let others come on board. MLK, Jr. was incredibly talented; however, if he had not allowed others to join his cause, the civil rights movement might have died with him! By bringing other people on board, he was able to accomplish so much more than he could ever have done on his own!

The easiest way for people to want to join your mission is for them to see your mission in action. What does that mean? People want to see you living your passion in everyday life. The easiest way for me to put this is in an example. Let's say that you own a gym. You are passionate about this gym. You want everyone you know to come and workout in your gym. You tell everyone how amazing your gym is, and how it has all the best equipment, all the best trainers, all the best classes. No gym in the world can compare with it. You tell everyone you meet about this gym. You tell them that if they go to any other gym, they are wasting their money. You talk about your gym with every breath that comes out of your mouth. Heck, I even want to join this gym, because of how highly you talk about it. You have the passion and mission for your gym but also a problem. You, the owner of this gym, are 200 pounds overweight! Why is that a problem? The problem has nothing to do with the actual pounds and everything to do with what those pounds represent! You are a walking billboard to the effectiveness of your product (in this case, your gym.) What does you being massively overweight say about your gym? It says one of two things: either that you will not get good results from being a member of the gym (stay overweight), or that you, the owner, do not even utilize your "amazing" product. Both of these are extremely negative to the effectiveness of your passion! How can it be that great if you are not willing to do it yourself? This brings to mind an old saying "Who you are speaks so loudly that I can't hear what you are saying." It means very little what you say. What matters the most is how you live your life! People will want to join your cause, your mission, only when they see you living it out in your own life! Are you living your passion out every day, or are you just telling people about it? MLK, Jr. lived his passion in every second of every day. He would not even have to tell you about his mission and you would want to be part of it, because how he lived spoke so loudly he did not even have to say anything! In what ways can you become more like that? Where in your life are you just talking about your passion, instead of living it?

The last thing to talk about is your legacy. This, for me, is the most important thing in the world. How will people remember me? Will they remember me for my core principles and values?

Will they remember me for all the work I did to expand my mission in life? Will they remember me at all?

I was talking about legacy with some friends of mine the other day. We were talking about future generations and the impact our lives will have on them. My hope and prayer is that in 5 or 6 or 20 generations down the road, my future family will not only still be talking about me (because that does not really matter) but actually still fighting my battle! In 200 years, will my offspring (and the people they influence) be continuing my work even though I am long gone? Hopefully they will. If that is my goal, then how do I live my life today to make that a reality tomorrow? Living my life with all the passion I have, never leaving my mission, not allowing complacency to set in, never being okay with the status quo, never stopping my calling and always pushing for a better tomorrow will ensure my legacy will be a lasting one. Do you want to be remembered? For how long do you want to be remembered? Will people not only want to continue what you are doing, but also want to be like you long after you are gone? If not, then what do you need to do RIGHT NOW to change into that person? Who do you have to become to make that a reality? The truth is that every person reading this book has the potential for that reality to be your life. You only have to decide to change, to make it your life, to have that happen! Are you going to choose to change? Or, are you going to choose to stay the same? The choice, as always, is yours!

CONCLUSION

You made it! You reached the end! You have everything you need to take over your life and reinvigorate your situation. With the strategies in place that you learned over the last 12 chapters, you are ready to not only change your own life, but start applying these trainings and resources to help others change. You have a choice to make. Either you can apply what you have learned and make massive life and success transformation, or this can be another book that just lines your bookshelf. You can choose either option! What are you going to choose?

If I know you at all (which by now, I think it is fair to assume you are different from all the people who would never read a book like this), you are more than ready to make a change for the better. The first thing you learned was how to "Diagnose the Problem." Now that you have the discovered the obstacles that are blocking your path to success, you can remove them to create a clear trajectory to your dreams. If you continue to use the exercises that we went through in the first part of this book, you will always have tools to overcome any future challenges that show up (because new ones will come, the question is, what will you do when they do show up?).

The second learning experience you received from this book was about "Cultivating Your Character." All the training resources that you were given in this part of the book will be massively important in order for you to develop into the type of person who creates success with every decision! The Time Map that you created will give you so much more time and efficiency that you will be able to get more work done, and in the process, move up the ladder to increased prosperity and success. The visualization and affirmations that you are using now will ensure that you are ready for the challenges that each day brings, and also help you manifest your dreams and build your day around how you want it to go, instead of going with the flow (which rarely works out for anyone).

Lastly, you learned about how to "Deliver the Goods." We walked through how to "Discover Your Passion." You were given different ways to assess what you are passionate about, and in the process learned what you could (and probably should) do for a career. By doing what you are passionate about, you will, without a doubt, be hugely successful. Any time you live a life of pursuing your passion, success HAS to follow! With following your passion, we also talked about going "all-in." With any passion, it is all consuming, and because of that, you will WANT to devote everything you have to fulfilling your passion. You learned exercises that will help you cultivate your ability to jump into the deep end without "Toeing the Water."

You were given the method for "Becoming a Master." You know now that it takes time (10,000 hours) to develop your skills to the level of master. You also know great joy exists in the process of becoming a master. Be excited with the process! Every day you are growing, adapting, changing, developing and becoming a better version of you. People will start noticing this change and want what you have! Let them come to you. Make sure you stay humble and remember your beginnings!

You have been shown the most important concept that has ever been taught..."Changing Your Culture"! This principle is crucial to getting your mission, dreams and goals accomplished. This vital component of the book walked you through how to let others join your mission. You can accomplish so much more with the help of others than you ever could on your own. Let others join you! There has never been a great movement or mission accomplished by the work of one person! Even Jesus needed the apostles and disciples to accomplish the Great Commission!

Finally, our greatest capacity to change comes after we start teaching others how to change. You can help a lot of people with the information that you received from this resource book! Will you step out to help another person? How can you, by stepping out for another person, change her life for the better? This may be the exact thing she needs to change her circumstances for the better. You could be the medium of growth that your friend or peer (or even a stranger) needs in order to save their house, their job, their marriage, etc. Will you be their saving grace? Will you keep this moving forward? This book could change so many lives...but only if you take the initiative to reach out to others!!

Thank you for reading. If you learned anything from this book, I hope it was that life is a continual learning process. We never arrive. We keep striving and moving forward to a better tomorrow. When we stop learning, we start moving away from our dreams and aspirations! Please, do not let that happen. We need you. This country needs you! Your friends and family need you. Stay thirsty!

ABOUT THE AUTHOR

Dr. Jake has worked with people professionally for the last 5 years, but this has been in his blood since he was a young boy. He has always wanted to help people and now he gets to everyday. He has worked with over 15,000 people in a one-on-one basis. He has also done 100's of seminars to thousands of people all over the country.

That experience has shaped him into the person he is today...a high energy, high impact, high flying, fun, family guy with a heart for people! He has taught thousands of people to overcome fear, love life, and live out their dreams!

To connect with Dr. Jake you can read more at his blog. http://www.JustAskDrJake.com

Dr. Jake Schmitz